Loosely Based
On A Made-Up Story

Loosely Based On A Made-Up Story

James Blunt

CONSTABLE

CONSTABLE

First published in Great Britain in 2023 by Constable

3 5 7 9 10 8 6 4

A CIP catalogue record for this book
is available from the British Library.

ISBN: 978-1-40871-562-8 (hardback)
978-1-40871-563-5 (trade paperback)

Typeset in Sabon LT Std by SX Composing DTP, Rayleigh, Essex
Printed and bound in Great Britain by Clays Ltd, Elcograf S.p.A.

Papers used by Constable are from well-managed forests
and other responsible sources.

Constable
An imprint of
Little, Brown Book Group
Carmelite House
50 Victoria Embankment
London EC4Y 0DZ

An Hachette UK Company

www.hachette.co.uk

www.littlebrown.co.uk

For Sofia – to whom all this led.

With my sister, Emily, who is four years older than me.

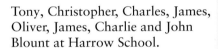

Tony, Christopher, Charles, James, Oliver, James, Charlie and John Blount at Harrow School.

At Elstree Preparatory School.

Front row: Officer Cadet Croft.
Middle row: Officer Cadets
Simpson, Na Nakhorn, Gordon.
Back row: Officer Cadet Shortarse.

I was callsign Three Zero.
The letter preceding your
callsign changes depending
on the Battle Code of the
day – so I'd be Foxtrot
Three Zero one day, or
perhaps Bravo Three Zero
the next.

Sensibly, The Blues & Royals tuck the
chinstrap under their chin. The Life Guards,
on the other hand, secure it under their
bottom lip. Imagine that at a sitting trot . . .

Recording electric guitar on *Back to Bedlam*.

'Take this down – I'll have one burrito, one hummus to share and some deep-fried pretzels.'

In rehearsals with producer Tom Rothrock prior to recording *Back to Bedlam* in 2003.

In the vocal booth for *Back To Bedlam*.

With Ahmet Ertegun, the founder of Atlantic Records.

Recording the demo to '1973' with Mark Batson.

Number 1, baby!

My manager, Todd Interland.

This Guy had a chopper that my sister Emily couldn't resist.

Sofia Wellesley visits the tour for the first time. Next time round, she would be Sofia Blount.

At my sister Emily's 40th birthday. This picture was taken a few minutes after my father told us that he had Stage 4 chronic kidney disease. Daisy is pregnant with her first child.

Billy's stag do before the ecstasy took hold.

Bobble is a babe magnet.

Ben Castle, John Garrison, Elton, me, Gary Pratworth and Beardy.

I bought my dad a kit aeroplane. It came in ten thousand pieces, and although I never expected him to actually build it, he did, in about eighteen months, and now we have to fly in it with him.

Producer Charlie Wessler on Carrie's porch. Charlie lived in Cabin No.1.

Carrie the day after my wedding.

The Prozac Pill that Carrie's ashes were buried in.

Carrie Fisher, Debbie Reynolds and Carrie's brother Todd.

Sylvain Bitton, the owner of Les Deux nightclub in West Hollywood.

Preface

I am a one-hit wonder. I know this, because when I walk down the street, strangers call out, 'Hey James! You're Beautiful!' I try to act all blasé, and say, 'Ha! I know what you did there . . .' but really, I'm thinking, 'Cunts!' It's worth realising though, that when you shouted, 'I don't believe it!' at Victor Meldrew, or 'Know what I mean, 'arry?' at Frank Bruno, they might have smiled back, but they thought you were cunts too. But whilst my crimes against music are well documented, I've got some stories that are not, and so I thought I'd write them down for your amusement and my parents' horror. Bearing in mind, much of this happened back in the musically utopian, drug-addled haze of the greatest decade in the history of mankind – The Naughties – and so, as Big Liz would say, recollections may vary.

It's also worth noting that where others change the names to protect the innocent, I've kept the names and embellished

the facts – kind of like the *Daily Mail*. So, while some of what follows is true, most is not. In fact, my lawyer is demanding I go further and clarify that none of this actually happened. The truth is not The Truth, and that's as honest as I can be. It's partially true, rather than painfully true, and I have possibly been economical with the truth, Your Honour.

One final disclaimer – I read that book by that Rolling Stone, where he said he was in a car that was stopped by the police, and in it were more drugs than you can imagine, but I live in Ibiza, and a guy turned up there with a lorry full of drugs, which is more than you can fit in a car. So either the Rolling Stone thinks you have a small imagination, or showing off about drugs is an important part of these books, so I've made up a lorry load of drug-related stories which, for my parents' sake, you should understand is me just trying to be cool, when we all know I'm not – except perhaps under fire.

The Blount Family

While most people are borne of four grandparents, I am from Norfolk, and like other Norfuckians, am descended from only two. What little I knew of my grandfather – he died when I was five – was that he was an orphan and that my grandmother was his cousin. He fought in the Second World War in Palestine, Syria and North Africa, had a lung burnt out at El Alamein, and where I have only two medals hanging on the wall, he had many, including the Military Cross.

Of my grandmother, I knew more. She was an eccentric woman called Polly who kept a sheep and a muntjac in her house. Neither deer, nor sheep, nor Polly were particularly house-trained, and one of them we eventually ended up eating for Sunday lunch. She tasted awful.

Perhaps because she was very old and all her friends had died, Polly's best friend was a large doll called Lucy. Lucy was about the size of a ten-year-old child and Polly had stitched her to a saddle, which she would strap to a Shetland pony called Shergar. She'd then lead them both round to the paddock at the rear of the house, whack the pony's arse and watch with glee as Shergar and Lucy would tear off, Lucy's arms and body flailing, over the jumps. My granny was nuts.

When Polly eventually died of dementia in my aunt's house in Dorset, my father put her in the boot of his Volvo and drove her back up to Norfolk to be buried. My dad's practical like that, but it did cause a little commotion at the service station. In death, we have kept only one of her letters. In it, she complained that her teeth were in awful condition, and as a result, she was finding it hard to masturbate.

As my relations are all fairly inbred, I didn't introduce any of them to my wife until we were married. She and I signed the marriage certificate at the Chelsea Registry Office, and then took a helicopter to Hampshire where they were all waiting to meet her, but by then it was too late.

Cousin Christopher

Cousin Christopher spoke in a slow, monotone voice, had a slightly oversized tongue, and was bullied at school by my father. They were both at Harrow-on-the-Hill, where generations of men from my family have been sent. Christopher once famously broke both his legs on the school farm by getting run over by a tractor that he was driving. When he missed the evening roll call, they sent out a search party and found him lying in agony in the dark, beside a gate, with the tractor some distance away in a ditch. He had apparently jumped off the tractor, intentionally leaving it in gear, so that he could open the gate, watch it drive through of its own accord, and jump back on. His remount, however, had not gone to plan, and he'd found himself under rather than on the tractor, thus crushing his legs.

Years later, Cousin Christopher became a trainspotter, and aged fifty-eight, died on a train whilst on an interrailing holiday in France, which is a bit like when base jumpers die doing

5

what they love. Cousin Christopher knew the risks. A French policeman phoned our home in Hampshire on a rainy evening to deliver the news. Apparently, Christopher had had a heart attack, but for some reason his body hadn't been taken off the train and the embarrassed policeman explained that they didn't know exactly where he was, except that he was dead. It was a Friday, and he was confident that his body would show up on Monday, perhaps in Lost & Found. With the difficult news delivered, the policeman paused and, seemingly unsure how best to say it, suggested that it might be an idea if we phoned Christopher's mobile, just in case anyone answered.

His job done, the policeman hung up, and we huddled round my father in his study as he dialled Christopher's number. It rang for what seemed like an age, and no one picked up, so my father left a message:

'Hello Christopher, it's Cousin Charles here. Sorry to hear you've died. Listen, if by any chance you get this message, would you call us back, please? We'd love to hear from you.'

Christopher never did call back, and sure enough they found him in a morgue on Monday in Marseille, which was the end of the line, in every way.

That said, it turns out repatriating bodies is eye-wateringly expensive, so my father had Cousin Christopher cremated in Marseille, and had his ashes DHL'ed home. He's practical like that.

Cousin Emma

Cousin Emma studied at the London School of Supernatural Ministry. There, for a fee, Emma learnt how to perform miracles. It was money well spent – in January 2019, another student prayed for Emma's leg to grow, and right then and there, it grew five millimetres. Up until that moment, Emma hadn't even known one of her legs was shorter than the other. Growing legs is the School of Supernatural Ministry's go-to miracle. Emma says that was the sixth time she'd seen them grow a leg. She is also getting the hang of it herself. After she commanded it to, her friend's leg grew two whole inches, and then shortened an inch, all in the course of five minutes. It must be in the family, as I've seen similar things happen to parts of my body in about the same length of time – but never a leg.

Cousin James

When I went to school, we had craft, design and technology classes, which were glorified woodwork lessons. By half-way through my first term, I had produced a small wooden bookshelf that sat on a flat surface and could support about eight books. In the same time, Cousin James made an aeroplane. Not a toy or a model. A real aeroplane. He didn't have a pilot's licence, and couldn't fly, so he was allowed to take it to the games pitches to run it up a little, but no more. Cousin James taxied the aircraft up and down the pitches a few times, and it seemed to work well. Eventually, however, he became impatient, and with no one watching, he decided to try to take off. He got it up to speed, pulled back on the stick, and sure enough, it flew — but at about fifty feet up, the nose too high, he stalled it. The plane fell out of the sky and crashed, and Cousin James broke just about every bone in his body. The first person to find him, almost dead, was a nurse, and only because of her did he live to

tell the tale. He'd started the day at five-foot-ten tall. He ended it at five-foot-eight, and in need of one of Cousin Emma's miracles.

On a serious note, Cousin James has recently developed a jet-powered seaplane and is looking for investors – in case you're interested.

Colonel Charles Blount

O n 6th November 1993, Riddick Bowe and Evander Holyfield fought at Caesars Palace in Las Vegas. During the match, which Holyfield would go on to win, a man called James Miller, flying a paramotor, attempted to land in the ring. Miller landed on the ropes, was dragged from the ring, and beaten unconscious by the baying crowd. Now, where most people thought Miller was an idiot, my father was inspired, and the next day went out and bought a paramotor for himself.

In many ways, this was not unexpected. My father became an army helicopter pilot when they'd only just invented helicopters. He was recognisable in our village for riding around on a penny-farthing, and was famous for attempting to waterski down the village stream whilst being towed behind a car, driven by my mother. He broke his leg in the attempt. He also dislocated his shoulder trying to barefoot waterski in an estuary, and he's only got eight fingers, as he lost two in a lawnmower.

Loosely Based On A Made-Up Story

When my father brought the paramotor home, I went to watch him teach himself how to fly it on a small hillock behind the house. It was a sight. With noisy, heavy motor, protective cage and propellor spinning on his back, he attempted to run down the slope, parachute trailing limply behind. Just as the chute looked like it might fill, he tripped and fell face down in the ground, accidentally hitting the throttle as he did. This in turn sent the engine screaming to full revolutions and the propellor spinning furiously, so drilling him face down, groaning, into the mud. He soon featured in the *Daily Express* under the headline, 'Rare Breeds', which sounds a lot like 'Inbreeds'. Perhaps they were being kind, as an alternative headline might easily have been 'Pillock on the Hillock'.

This was not his first foray into self-taught flying. In 1976, my father entered the first ever Hang-Gliding World Championships, having just taught himself on the ancient hills of Watership Down. His friend, Tommy Collins, with whom he'd bought the newly invented contraption, read out the instructions on how to build it:

'Stick pole A into joint B,' he'd shout, 'then joint B into pole C,' and so on until he got to the instruction, 'Point into wind . . . Run . . . Jump!' On that first flight, my father broke his nose and bit through his tongue, but as he was fairly accident-prone, this was considered a good result.

The first Hang-Gliding World Championships were in the Alps in Austria, and rather than run down the hill to take off, competitors wore skis and took off from the snow. There weren't many rules, except that competitors had to fly through a course of Zeppelin balloons, and then try to land on a cross marked on

the ground. Whoever landed nearest the cross would win. Of all the competitors, Terry DeLore from New Zealand completed the slalom successfully, but realising he was overshooting the cross, stalled his hang-glider. He fell from a great height, landed bang-smack in the middle of the cross, breaking both legs as he did, but was crowned Hang-Gliding World Champion.

My father came 109th.

And I should tell you more about why my father has only eight fingers, which has nothing to do with him coming from Norfolk. When I was seventeen, I was mowing the lawn at my parents' house and accidentally clipped a tree, which knocked off the front-right wheel. The lawnmower is hard to restart when it's hot, but with safety in mind, I cut the engine and put the wheel back on. About three weeks later, my father mowed the lawn, and towards the end of the job, the wheel fell off again. He was only a few metres from finishing, and so rather than cut the motor, he lifted the side of the mower with his left hand to attach the wheel with his right. His hand came back with two fingers missing.

Perhaps a little embarrassed, my father wrapped the injured hand in a dishcloth, packed an overnight bag for himself, sent a couple of emails and switched off the computer – we know this because of the blood on the mouse and keyboard – and took my youngest sister round to the neighbours'. Against my father's wishes – he was adamant he could do it himself – the neighbour drove him to hospital.

After the accident, I was the first one home and was tasked with finding the fingers before the dog did. They had been swept into the bag with the grass cuttings at the back of the mower,

but not before the blades had puréed them. The only things still intact were his two fingernails, which I kept for posterity. The fingers, however, were unusable, so I dug a small, shallow grave by the woodshed and buried them, saying as I did, 'Dear God. Here's the first instalment of my father. Please let me keep the rest of him for a bit longer.'

My father was a colonel in the Army Air Corps at the time, and members of his regiment went to visit him in hospital, bringing gifts like Cadbury's Chocolate Fingers, and as he was the commanding officer, they soon adopted a new regimental salute with the ring and middle fingers tucked away.

My father recently found himself in hospital again with stage 4 chronic kidney disease and in need of a new kidney. I had just had an unwanted child, and so tried to give him one of its kidneys, but sadly it wasn't a match. He was still grateful for the gesture. I wrote him a song called 'Monsters', which got played on the radio, and as a result he was given a total of fourteen kidneys, some of which we still have on ice, and others we sold for a small profit. Remarkably, the one we ended up using was given to him by a man also called Charles Blount. Nervous that this might cause a mix-up during surgery, I wrote 'GIVER' in permanent marker on one Charles's forehead and 'TAKER' on the other.

My father has always been apologetic that he didn't die, so that the song would have been a bigger hit. In fact, a boy in America, whose daddy had just died a month earlier, sang the song on a TV show called *American Idol*, and the song went to number three in the charts, so my daddy was right. We plan to re-release it when he does.

Jane Ann Farran Blount

My mother is an Amazonian woman whom we call the Command Module. She has shoulders broader than an Olympic swimmer, and it is from her that I inherited my impressive physique. She also brings some much-needed diversity to the monotone gene pool of my Norfuckian roots. Whilst she claims to be Church of England, she is in fact Jewish – her maiden name is Amos – and as a child, she fed me only liver. We are very close, despite the beatings.

She was tough on me as a child. I had to call both her and my father 'sir'. If I failed to eat dinner, the same plate of food was produced for breakfast the next day. It is worth noting that she is also the person who made me – not just in body, but in conscience too. I owe her everything, and she will always be my unsung hero. She made me take up the violin when I was four years old, and with a group of other children, made us play 'Hot-Crossed Buns' whilst dancing in an anti-clockwise direction around a lone bun. A few years later, I learnt that this was some kind of satanic ritual and that that kind of thing was pretty rife in the seventies. She is also the one who told me my music was crap long before any of you, and in doing so, equipped me with Komodo-like skin.

She was witness to my first ever car crash, in Nicosia, Cyprus, in a powder-blue Citroën 2CV. I was driving the car and I was aged four. We lived on an army patch with the United Nations, and our garage was open at the back as well as the front – more like a lean-to than a garage. The open back led into our gently sloping garden, at the end of which was a post and rail fence, and beyond that, a minefield.

The car was parked in the garage, and knowing that we were about to leave the house, I had climbed into the front passenger seat while my mother locked up. At four years old, I knew the difference between the gearstick and the handbrake, and so thought nothing of wiggling the former whilst avoiding the latter. What I was about to learn is that you can leave a car in gear and not apply the handbrake – something my parents did often, it turns out. The car slipped gently out of gear, and slowly at first, began rolling forwards out of the back of the garage and into the garden. From there it began picking up speed down the grassy slope towards the fence and minefield beyond.

Fairly early on in what I assumed would be the car's final journey, I bailed out. I knew that whatever happened in the next few seconds, my arse was going to be very sore as soon as my father got home, and pre-empting that, I thought it best to start apologising immediately.

'Mummy! I'm sorry! I'm sorry!' I screamed.

Within a millisecond, and like a fullback in hot pursuit of the breakaway winger, my mother came sprinting out of the kitchen door. For a minute, the two seemed equally matched. But by about halfway down the garden, the car got the upper hand and the distance started to widen. Realising this was the last chance, my mother leapt, arms outstretched, attempting what looked like a late ankle-tap tackle. It was a fantastic and terrible sight: the car bouncing its way to oblivion; my mother suspended in mid-air; and me on the sidelines already in tears, watching in terror after what had been, in my mind, a fairly innocuous wiggle of a gearstick. There was a moment of hope as my mother, now descending more rapidly towards the ground, managed to get the fingertips of both hands on to the bumper and, even as her body hit the ground, take what looked like a solid hold.

But the car had the momentum.

With my mother now being dragged behind it, the car careered on, veering side to side slightly as it reached fence-breaking speed. At the moment it occurred to me that, at four years old, I was responsible for killing both the car and my mother – and wondering what the punishment for THAT was – a miracle happened. At the bottom of the garden, only a metre from the wooden fence, was a metal washing line pole. Its position had always looked so random, but suddenly it seemed as if it had been placed with all the forethought of Nostradamus. The car ran dead centrally into it. The flimsy aluminium front bumper crumpled and the 2CV's fold-up windows detached themselves from the car and flew over the fence into the minefield . . . but fantastically the car was stopped, dead in its tracks, and my mother alive, although dusty, in hers.

eBay

I have two sisters, one of whom, twelve years younger than me, was a mistake. Having a sense of humour, and because she was a whoops-a-daisy, my parents called her Daisy. My other sister, Emily, I sold on eBay in 2005.

It was around the time that I was about to go on my first world tour and so had been clearing out my flat on the Fulham Palace Road by auctioning everything I owned on the website. I had returned to my near-empty flat one day to find my sister, who lived with me, crying on the floor. She explained that she couldn't get to a funeral in Cork in time as the planes were on strike and the ferries were out of season. Seeing a business opportunity, and knowing it's a seller's market, I put her on eBay under the headline, 'Damsel in distress, needs knight in shining armour to save the day'. In the subtext, I explained the problem, and used the best picture I could find. To my surprise, different people bid and bid, until one won. The man who won had a helicopter, so he could fly her to the funeral, and amazingly they started dating and are now married.

The man concerned is called Guy Harrison, and he happens to be the man who threw the purple-powdered condom that hit Tony Blair in the House of Commons. That's why they have protective glass screens in the public gallery now. Guy was in an organisation called Fathers 4 Justice and had had a shitty experience where his then girlfriend, who sounds like a psychopath, told him she had cancer and needed money for treatment, but then got pregnant. When Guy dug a little deeper, he found paperwork that showed she didn't have cancer at all, but had used his money for hormone treatment to get pregnant. Guy confronted her, told her she was batshit crazy, and soon after, they split. For three years, his now ex-girlfriend allowed him access to the child, but then she met someone else, moved up north and cut Guy off, even sending back all the Christmas and birthday presents he'd send his young daughter.

The law courts insisted numerous times that the mother allow Guy access, even saying they'd send her to prison if she didn't, but she ignored them, and in reality, they don't send young mothers to prison for that anyway. When his daughter turned sixteen, Guy got a private detective to hand her a letter explaining that he was her father, and his side of the story. From a distance, the detective watched her read it, but even then, she didn't get in touch, and soon after that, he heard she'd been illegally taken to Australia.

A couple of years later, I became a judge on *The X Factor* in Australia with Danni Minogue and Chris Isaak. Us being judges was a bit ironic really. Chris only knows music from before the fifties, I only know my own music, and Danni doesn't even like music. But by some weird coincidence, my brother-in-law found out that a girl called Marlisa, who was in his daughter's class in Sydney, had won the competition the year before. Now, each year, in the live finals of the programme, the previous year's winner comes on the show and sings, so Guy asked me if, when Marlisa made her appearance, I would ask her if she knew his daughter. This was a terrible idea – performers are kept away from us backstage, and I was only going to be able to speak to her when the judges take to the stage immediately after her performance – a moment that is broadcast live to millions of people. I explained this to Guy, but he was desperate, and so I reluctantly agreed to give it a try. Well, the young girl sang, and when she finished, we all stood up and clapped, and then the four judges climbed on the stage. Pop star Guy Sebastian asked her how a year in the spotlight had been, and Danni Minogue said she had grown as a performer, and Chris Isaak told her she was really pretty.

Then I asked her in a low voice if she knew a girl called Izzy Thornton-Bott from her class and, at that moment, the whole world stopped and everyone on the stage and the audience and down the TV at home looked at me like *WTF!?* – especially Marlisa – and as they cut to commercial, I was left standing there thinking, *Fuck how, on national television, did I become that guy your parents warned you about?*

Elstree School

Aged seven years old, my parents sent me to an all-boys boarding school. The first I knew of this was when they bought me a Nintendo Donkey Kong Game & Watch. It was neither Christmas nor my birthday, and I sensed something was up. That afternoon, they drove me to Elstree Preparatory School in Woolhampton, Berkshire.

On the first floor, at the end of a long, uncarpeted corridor above what looked like an old stable block, I was led into a room where eight other children were watching television. As it turned out, that would be the only time in five years at the school that I would see either that room or a television. I sat on the sofa and played with my Game & Watch, and a few minutes later, my parents put their heads round the door to mouth, 'Goodbye,' and with that, they left. It was 6th September 1982.

Three days later, I asked the matron, who was the closest thing to a real-life witch that can exist in a seven-year-old's mind, when my parents were coming back. 'At Christmas,' she cackled.

In the end, my parents didn't get in touch again till I was famous.

At boarding school, there are occasional weekends, called Exeats, when pupils are allowed home. On those weekends, the whole school would empty, but by now my father was based in Germany, so I remained at school with two other children whose parents were in Singapore. If there is a positive to take from this, it is that I am happy in my own company – although others might describe me as a loner, or sociopath.

We slept in dormitories with up to twelve boys in each and, closely watched by the duty master, washed twice a week in communal showers. Living in such close proximity to a hundred and seventy other children, the only place one might be alone was either in the loo cubicles or the music practice rooms, so I took up the piano, because back then at least, I didn't enjoy hanging out in loos.

Although I joke about beatings and buggery at boarding school, both only happened once, and not at the same time. We had been on a school trip to an Iron Age museum, and as the tour of the museum ended, we were left for some minutes in the souvenir shop. Here, a group of the cooler kids amongst us began shoplifting. There were only trinkets and cheap tat, but one of the women working in the shop saw what was going on and pointed the thieves out to a master. Each boy that had been fingered by the woman was taken aside, the stolen articles retrieved, and the miscreant told he would be seeing the headmaster on our return to school. It was an ominous bus ride back. Halfway home, the master in charge came and sat beside me and said that he'd seen me amongst the thieves. Had I stolen anything? he asked. I had. I'd stolen a faux leather money-holder worth two pounds fifty. Realising I was busted, I admitted my crime, but told the master that when I'd seen the woman speaking to him, I'd put the purse back on the shelf from which it came. In actual fact, I'd stuffed it down the back of my pants and was currently sitting on it.

Mr. McMullen, the headmaster, gave each thief six of the best with the cane, but as I'd apparently returned the item, I received only three. We all met in the changing rooms afterwards, some tearful, others more cheerful, and one by one pulled down our trousers and pants to compare welts. When it was my turn, as I pulled my trousers down, the cheap faux leather purse fell to the floor and to cheers and everyone's great admiration, there was not a mark on my arse.

In five years of prep school, my only real achievement was being cast as Jim in the school production of *Treasure Island*, but an hour before the performance, I knocked myself out whilst swinging on a door lintel in the loos. I'd been trying to push people into the urinal with my feet, but swung too high, lost grip and hit my head on the stone floor. Unconscious and convulsing on the floor, the other boys started shouting, 'Fake! Fake! Fake!' until Jonathan Sidebottom pointed out that my feet were actually in the urinal. Everyone fled, except the kindly Sidebottom, who went to fetch a teacher.

An ambulance took me to hospital, where I spent the next three nights. I didn't feel that sorry for myself – in the bed beside me was a young boy whose emergency circumcision had gone wrong, and his penis was now the size of a grapefruit.

My sole other accolade was being awarded the Prefect's Reading Prize, for which I was given a leather-bound *Good News Bible* on the final day of school. I sold it five minutes after prize-giving for eight pounds, but the kid who'd bought it off me told his parents, and they drove back to school and told the headmaster. This was a real crush on my entrepreneurial spirit, and perhaps the moment I decided to diverge towards music.

Harrow-on-the-Hill

Aged thirteen, like my father, and his father, and his father before him, I was sent to Harrow-on-the-Hill. The school is, as the name suggests, on a hill in northwest London, overlooking the less affluent South Harrow below. Interactions with local youths were abrasive. We were a bunch of stuck-up little toffs dressed in morning coats and boater hats and were considered sport for the locals.

Once, when it had snowed, thirty of us had a snowball fight with fifty locals in the graveyard by the church. Initially we threw snowballs, but then both sides started adding ice and stones to the mix. At some point, Robin Fox, son of the actor James and brother of that prat Laurence, got too close to our opponents.

One of them – we'll call him Kevin – pointed to some blood on the ground, and in an accent of your choice said, 'Is that one of your blokes' blood or one of ours?'

In a crystal-clear up-his-own-arse accent, with a dash of disdain in his tone, Robin replied, 'It's certainly not ours. Our blood is blue.'

Whereupon Kevin and his mates proceeded to kick the shit out of him.

Seeing this, with a rousing 'Come on, chaps! Follow me!' I summoned the other Harrovians, ran towards the nearest of Kev's friends, smacked him in the face, and looking back for support, saw that no one had followed me.

That was the first time my nose was broken.

Years later, I would go on to break my nose again when I was skiing with the army. It was New Year's Eve, when thirty thousand people gather in the Place Centrale in Verbier in the Swiss Alps. Sometime after midnight, when the square was a mess of drunk, rowdy Brits and Swiss, Brigadier Montgomery's daughter, Amber, stumbled over to me with her knickers round her ankles. She'd just had a pee behind a building and was having difficulty getting them back up. I bent over to help, but as I did, a crowd of young men surged towards her exposed bottom, shoving her forward towards me so that our heads hit, knocking me clean out. I came round alone, with the taste of blood in my mouth, a painful misshaped nose and two black eyes, thinking to myself, *Well . . . that's the last time I offer to pull a girl's knickers up.*

Public schools generally have their own language. In my first year at Harrow, called a Shell, I was assigned to a sixth-form Fagmaster, for whom I had to work as his Special. I was to refer to him only as 'God'. I woke him up each morning with a cup of coffee and toast, drew his curtains, made his bed and did his laundry. He paid me fifteen pounds each term and would buy me cigarettes and three cans of beer on weekends. He would also get me out of trouble if I fell out of favour with other members of the top year. Sixth Formers would enter the Shell dormitory lines calling, 'Boy! Boy! Boy!' and whoever arrived last was given whatever task the more senior pupil needed doing. Junior boys could be given Skews – black marks – by Sixth Formers. Three Skews and you'd get Jerks, which involved being taken on a forced run to the playing fields at 6 a.m. on Sunday morning and getting generally Beasted. The senior boys present would concoct various unpleasantries, like making us run through ditches of nettles in our shorts or doing long jump into the frozen lake.

The initiation ceremony for Shells was pretty out-there. It took place on the second floor, in the Head of House's bedroom. Inside, the twelve or so members of the top year had gathered, drinking beer. New boys lined up outside and were called in, in pairs. There were some light-hearted bits:

'Do you have a girlfriend?' they'd ask.

At fourteen years old, I was four-foot-ten and had barely even spoken to a girl.

'Er, yes,' I replied unconvincingly.

'What's her name?' someone asked.

'Umm, Morag,' I stuttered.

'BULLSHIT!' they all brayed, throwing empty cans at me.

And so it went on, my co-initiate being asked similar questions.

But the bit where they made the guy beside me drop his trousers and pants, and tie one end of a long, coiled up piece of string to his todger was more extreme. String attached, the

Head of House picked up a brick that was tied to the other end of the long coil . . . and threw it out of the window.

Held back against the wall by two seniors, the young boy screamed. The string rapidly uncoiled, chasing the brick out of the window. We expected it to suddenly go taut, taking his tackle with it, but before it could – BAM! – the brick hit the ground. The string was, as the seniors had designed, longer than the two-storey drop.

The Banned

In the second year at Harrow, called the Remove, you are no longer required to work for a Sixth Former, but have little going for yourself other than the ability to order round the Shells. It was at this time that I took up the electric guitar, learnt how to play 'Money for Nothing' by Dire Straits and announced that I was going to be a pop star. A pupil in the Lower Fifth, called Henry O'Bree, showed me the three chords I currently know. Henry went on to kill himself in a car while at university, aged just twenty, and I write his name more than anything to say I wish he'd known the gift he gave me.

There were early signs of the offence that I would go on to cause the nation: for the Inter-House Music Competition, my entry comprised of drums, bagpipes, and me on electric guitar and vocals, doing a mashup of 'Flower of Scotland', 'It's Grim Up North' by The Justified Ancients of Mu Mu (otherwise known as the KLF) and 'I Can't Walk' by Genesis. Throughout the performance, I had a nosebleed all over my bright yellow Japanese Fender Telecaster. We didn't win.

Around this time, I formed a band with my best friend, Rupert. Aged fourteen, Rupert didn't want to be in a band – he wanted to be a mercenary – but to humour me, he learnt some Jimi Hendrix solos, and played them over whatever I was playing – even if that was Eric Clapton's 'Wonderful Tonight' or Don McLean's 'American Pie'. He was also at a different school, so we never actually practised.

Rupert lived in the next-door village to me where I grew up in Hampshire. He was a wild and dangerous friend to have. Before we had driving licences, we stole his mother's car and drove to Basingstoke with his younger sister in the back to watch *Terminator 2*, very nearly dying whilst trying to cross the A303. He found neutral instead of a gear and we rolled slowly across the dual carriageway in the dark, narrowly avoiding being hit by oncoming traffic.

Anyway, we called the band 'The Banned', and my sister, Emily, secured us our first gig at St Mary's all-girls school in Wantage, where she was a pupil. I'd pulled in a drummer, keyboard player and backing singer, again all from different schools, and our first ever rehearsal was an hour before the gig. With hindsight, the whole thing was a bad idea. Boys from Radley School had been invited along to the dance and a DJ played after us, but they all soon realised we were crap. Halfway through the second song, the keyboard player accidentally hit the demo button, and 'Greensleeves' overrode whatever noise the rest of us were making. Rupert was still on the wah-wah pedal, shredding away, while we were on 'A Whiter Shade of Pale' and one of the Radley boys threw a bread roll, which I caught, took a bite from and threw back, halfway through the song – but that was the highlight. The Banned disbanded soon after.

Rupert never did go on to become a mercenary. Instead, after some minor brushes with law enforcement and the Mexican Zapatista militant group, he joined the British Special Forces and is currently a brigadier with an OBE and will probably end up being head of the British Army.

I was released from Harrow in July 1987 with A-levels in Physics, Chemistry and Economics. I didn't enjoy my time there – some people in my boarding house were horrible little turds and five years cooped up with them was pretty miserable – but I have still enrolled my children in the school, so that they might know my pain.

John Smith

I wasn't always going to become a musician. I considered becoming a lawyer instead. In fact, sometime after school, I did a week's work-experience with a law firm, visiting their chambers in London and watching different cases from the public gallery in the Royal Courts of Justice.

The first case I attended involved a man called John Smith, who was fifty years old, still lived with his parents, and was accused of buggering a cat on the Metropolitan line of the London Underground. Five witnesses had been called to testify against him, four of whom were in the carriage and had seen him drop his trousers round his ankles and stick the cat on his cock. The fifth testified to hearing a cat wailing in pain in the station after the event. A doctor also gave evidence, saying that on examination, he had found three cat hairs on Mr. Smith's penis – although in his defence, John claimed the hairs in question belonged to his parents' cats, and had got on his penis while he was sitting on the loo at home. Apparently, that's where they liked to sit too.

I didn't stay long enough to find out if they DNA'ed the cats and, you know, I'm not sure if cat DNA profiling was that advanced back then anyway.

After that, a bit like at Wimbledon, I moved to Court Number Two, where I sat and listened to the tragic story of two best friends who had taken a girl they both fancied into a forest one night. They'd built a fire, smoked cigarettes and drunk beer, but ended up fighting over her, and one had killed the other. The accused young man was full of remorse at the loss of his best friend at his own hands, and yet, throughout the truly harrowing testimony, the man sitting beside me in the public gallery was wanking. I decided that I didn't want to be a lawyer after all.

University of the West of England

After Harrow, I went on to study Aerospace Manufacturing Engineering – which I couldn't spell – at the University of the West of England. Now, Aerospace Manufacturing Engineering is not a fun course, and contrary to the whole point of university, required me to actually work. I spent my time studying stresses and strains of metals by bending them until they broke. While my friends on other courses had six hours of lectures a week, I had an ungodly thirty-six. To make matters worse, of the hundred and seventy people on my course, only three of them were girls – and I only realised the third was a girl when she got pregnant.

I lived in a one-bedroomed flat in Clifton with two other boys. Two of us slept in an L-shaped sitting room, and the other one got the bedroom. I'd stolen a condom machine from one of the university halls of residence and installed it in the bathroom, and we brewed mind-degradingly strong but foul-tasting beer in the kitchen. It was more bachelor slum than pad. My flatmates were both taking two-year HNDs – Higher National Diplomas – or, as we called them, Have No Degrees. One of my flatmates had taken five attempts to pass GCSE Maths and seven times to pass his driving test. He went on to become a plumber, but not one I would recommend.

My girlfriend at the time was at the intellectually superior University of Bristol, studying Sociology. Hers was a much more convenient six-hour-a-week course, and so, a month before the end of our first year, she took me to meet the professors in the Social Sciences Department on Woodland Road in the hope that they could possibly help me change not just my course, but also my university. There, I met with the Social Policy professor, which we all know is the lowest rung of the academic ladder. She was a stocky, shaven-headed woman who took an instant dislike to me – until I spelt out that I wanted to repent my spoilt, public-school background and give back to the community – starting by studying Social Policy. She told me she loved me and offered me an unconditional place, and in doing so, freed me of any requirement to pass my end-of-year exams back at the University of the West of England. Not only was she giving me a place at a better university, but a month's holiday as well.

When it came to it, I still took the Aerospace Manufacturing Engineering exams – just for fun. It was a requirement that you stayed for the first half hour, so I scribbled away frantically for the first thirty minutes of each three-hour exam, and then, bang on the thirtieth minute, put my pen away, stood up, gestured nonchalantly to imply the exam was easy, and walked out. The other students shat themselves. They needn't have worried. I got

5 per cent, 5 per cent, 11 per cent, 13 per cent and 15 per cent –
but was upgraded to Bristol University.

To the professor's dismay, I didn't stick with Social Policy. In
the first couple of weeks, I switched to Sociology and Philosophy.
Another six-hour-a-week course, it allowed me to watch both
Neighbours and *Home and Away* twice a day, and of the
hundred and seventy people on the course, three, including me,
were boys.

University of Bristol

Some weeks into my Sociology course, it became apparent that of the hundred and sixty-seven girls studying with me, all of them were vegans, and so, after much consideration, I became a carnivore. I lived only on chicken and mince, supplementing each with mayonnaise or ketchup respectively.

That said, like other revolutionaries before me, taking a stand is not always easy. A few weeks into my new dietary regime, I began to feel quite exhausted, and my limbs hurt almost constantly. When my gums started bleeding and my hair started falling out, I thought it best to see a doctor. He did some tests, raised a curious eyebrow and told me I had developed scurvy. Evidently, the vitamin content of condiments was not as much as I'd hoped.

Back on campus, my peers didn't call it scurvy. They called it toxic masculinity. But all new journeys hit bumps along the way, and armed with the knowledge that my dietary issues were basically just caused by a lack of vitamin C, I added a litre of orange juice to my daily intake.

Two weeks later, I ended back in the doctor's, and referred on to an ear, nose and throat specialist, who diagnosed me with acute acid reflux. Apparently too much orange juice is also bad for you, although they don't put that on the carton.

The doctor did ask about the sense in all this, and I still maintain that it is only by pushing ourselves that we evolve and grow. On tour, I once ate only tinned sweetcorn for two weeks, and although I'm unable to show you the result, when it came, it was a thing of great wonder.

The Lada

When I was nineteen, still at university and trying to attract members of the opposite sex, I bought my first car. It was a Lada. A Lada Riva SL to be exact – the SL was for 'slow'. She was Ferrari red, and I was told she'd had only one previous owner – an old woman who had died of natural causes. This confused me, as soon after I bought her, I found a condom, ready to go, Blu Tacked to the steering column. I installed an unnecessarily large sound system in the boot, covered the speakers on the back shelf with a tartan blanket, and insisted that my passengers wore brown bobble hats at all times. My sister was a member of the Brownies, so had a large collection of them. Although *Autocar* magazine said she should be able to reach eighty-one miles an hour, out of principle, I never took the car over fifty. I also attached an old metal roof rack for greater wind resistance. I waved overenthusiastically at other Lada drivers, and presumably borne of the same principle, they never waved back.

One evening, I parked the car outside Manor Hall in Clifton, and that night someone broke into her and stole the sound system. For me, the only thing less cool than owning a Lada is stealing from one. I sold her, for more than I'd bought her, to a Russian who shipped her back to the Motherland.

I now own an AC Cobra, which is an American muscle car. They set you back about a quarter of a million pounds. Mine, however, is a fake and cost me twenty grand, but having bought the low-slung sports car, in order to get it up to my home in Ibiza, I had to tarmac the track that leads to the house – at a cost of thirty grand. She is beautiful, and when I drive her, people wave and shout, 'Hey! David Guetta!'

My other car is a tuk-tuk, which I bought after a concert in Bangkok in 2008. Having hitched a ride on one, I had a pop star moment, took a picture of the little three-wheeled taxi, and sent it to my tour manager with a message saying, 'I'll have one of these, please!' He had it shipped to Ibiza and I drive my children to school in it every day. People on the side of the road wave me down and ask. 'How much is it to Ibiza Town, please?' and then when they recognise me, they go, 'Oh shit, man. What happened to you?'

The Plane Crash

I am a nervous passenger. I shouldn't be – my father was an army helicopter pilot, after all, and I got my private pilot's licence, through a Royal Air Force scholarship scheme, when I was sixteen, before I could even drive a car. But then again, most of my recent ancestors were pilots who have died in plane crashes.

There was a clue when I bought the airline tickets. The Aeroflot flight to Bangkok was half the price of all the other airlines. But I was a broke university student, and you kind of figure that they must be saving money on service rather than safety.

We'd got there safely enough, had spent time on the islands of Ko Pha-Ngan and Koh Tao, and danced till dawn on Hat Rin beach at the full-moon party, but now it was time for me and my girlfriend to return to London. In a few weeks, I would be joining the army, and now found myself in a tired-looking aircraft on a late-night flight with a girlfriend who had just eaten a lump of hash the size of a die, and was in the throes of paranoia. Just getting her onboard was hard enough. She was convinced something was wrong. As the plane started down the runway, she immediately started saying the plane was broken. She was extremely high and I tried to reassure her that it was just the hash. We were sitting in the central four seats, a few rows behind the wing, but through the darkness outside I could see the lights of the airport flash past at an ever-increasing rate. As we reached critical speed, she was starting to raise her voice in panic. I was struggling to calm her down, and then it struck me that although we were going fast, maybe she was right – it just didn't feel fast enough. The nose lifted, and we left the ground, and immediately everyone else realised something was wrong too. Instead of following a confident upwards trajectory, we travelled nose up, forwards but not upwards, like a water-skier unable to lift himself out of the water. And then, as if by way of explanation, the left engine blew up.

It looked like the sun had landed on the left wing. You couldn't see the flames – it was just burning, bright yellow all across the windows on the left. The aircraft gave up trying and started to fall. 'Brace! Brace! Brace!' was shouted over the Tannoy. We hit the ground hard and were thrown forwards. The seats folded forwards with us, compressing chests into legs. I heard screams, but most people were silent, overwhelmed by the sensory overload. The overhead lockers flew open, throwing their contents across the cabin, and as I looked forwards, I had a moment to think how weird it was to be in a metal cylinder, unable to see what's ahead, and wondering what it's going to look like when we hit whatever's ahead of us. Will the wall of the cockpit concertina backwards so we all just squash together? A minute earlier I'd been willing the plane to go faster. Now we were all desperately willing it to stop. Out of runway, the aircraft slew to the right and then, to our surprise, it came to a halt.

Two hundred seatbelts clicked open in unison. And then the fighting began.

So, you're in a confined space, with luggage and coats and crap everywhere, and outside, the whole left-hand side of the aircraft is on fire. Everyone is standing up, and everyone is literally fighting for their lives to get out. The two Italians boys behind us got up, left their girlfriends, and fought their way to the exit fifteen metres ahead of us, oblivious to the door three metres behind. The stewards and stewardesses stood up and started shouting for everyone to sit down, and the men nearest them stood up and punched them to the ground. Everyone fought to get past each other, in any direction, not knowing which way to go.

'How are we going to get out?' my girlfriend kept asking. I didn't know. It was just a mass of people and no space for anyone.

Anyway, it turns out I get quite chatty in an emergency.

'We need everyone to sit down,' I replied.

'We need everyone to sit down *now*,' I repeated. The need was desperate and panicked. But you can't just will something to happen, you have to make it happen.

'I need you all to sit down now,' I started saying more loudly.

And as the urgency and panic took over, uncontrollably, I became the voice of my father, telling the dog to sit when it was chasing a pheasant across a road.

'DOWN!' I was yelling. 'DOWN! SIT DOWN! NOW!'

And just like that, in the same way as the plane had just come to a halt, everyone sat down.

A hundred or so heads turned to me, like the dog, knowing they'd done something wrong, and waited for the next instruction.

'Thank you!' I said.

I sat down too.

The air hostesses stood up and gathered round the doors. They wouldn't open, but by now, fire engines were swarming round the plane and the sun on the wing was beginning to dim, replaced with a white foam, as if we were in a car wash.

It took them forty-five minutes to extract us.

The injured were taken to hospital in ambulances, and the rest taken to a five-star hotel in the centre of Bangkok. My girlfriend and I were in heaven. Not because we'd died, but because for the last month we'd lived on five pounds a day, sleeping in beach huts, and now here we were, bouncing up and down on the huge double beds and ordering room service, care of Aeroflot.

But three days later, and with a terrible sense of doom, Aeroflot staff put us on an identical plane, in the same seats, at the same time of night, to try the whole thing again. The Italian boys were sitting next to their now ex-girlfriends, and the only sound, other than the roar of engines as we took off, was sobbing.

In Moscow, we were taken by bus to a grey, Soviet hotel, escorted into lifts without buttons and operated only by someone with a key, and shown to a grey, dilapidated room. The next morning, we were flown back to the UK.

It seems a wasted sentence to say that I will never fly Aeroflot again.

Royal Military Academy Sandhurst

When I first went to university, I was awarded an Army Bursary. For this, the army gives you five hundred pounds each term, which my parents spent on slot machines in Andover, and in return, I was contracted to four years of military service.

Before enlisting, you must first pass a medical. And so, on leaving university, I reported to Tidworth Army Hospital in Hampshire, which by coincidence was the same hospital where I was born, some twenty-one years earlier. There, two Statler and Waldorf-like brigadiers told me to strip down to my boxers, which was an issue, as I go commando. Having no other option, I took off my jeans, shirt and socks and stood there, pale and naked. They asked me what exercise I did, and I told them I liked nightclubbing, and they took my weight, which came to a tasty sixty-two kilos. Homosexuality was illegal in the Armed Forces back then, and so after the standard cup-and-cough of my balls – rather than take one ball each, they took it in turns to hold both of them – then they made me bend over, and standing behind me, both men crouched down to inspect my ring for wear and tear.

'What do you think?' one said gruffly.

'It looks good to me!' the other exclaimed excitedly.

'Yes, it does, doesn't it!' said the first.

And with that, I was accepted into the Armed Forces.

A few weeks later, my father drove me to the Royal Military Academy Sandhurst to join Course 963 in a suit and carrying an ironing board. We parked on the parade ground, walked up the steps into Old College, shook hands and said goodbye. The instant the last parent had left, the colour sergeants started shouting.

'As you were!' they screamed. 'Get into three ranks! Platoon, platoon shun! Right turn! Left, right! Left, right!' and we were marched at an impossible speed to our company lines where we were to be housed. Each cadet was assigned a small brown and orange coloured room with a bed, cupboard and chest of drawers. As it would turn out, we didn't sleep in the beds, we slept on the floor beside them. And I didn't know it then, but including my time in Kosovo and Canada, it would be the first night of two years sleeping either on the floor or on the ground outside.

We were marched everywhere, as fast as the colour sergeants could machine gun the words 'left' and 'right' repetitively. At mealtimes, we were marched into the mess hall, and the moment we had retrieved our food from the servery and got close to putting the plate down on the table, we would be marched out again. On the first day, you had time for maybe a mouthful. By the second, because you moved a little faster, maybe two.

By the third day, you'd learnt to eat the entire plateful of food the moment it was handed to you, and go on a run immediately afterwards.

'You never know when the enemy is coming over the hill!' Colour Sergeant Morte would shout.

Your room at Sandhurst is a work of art: socks are rolled up identically in the drawers; shirts are ironed with the arms folded across each other and hung an inch apart in the cupboard; curtains are pleated and the bottoms folded on to the windowsill; and bedclothes are ironed into place with the folds in the sheets, from headboard to turndown, measured with a bible. It takes about forty-five minutes to prepare a room for the 6 a.m. inspection, so rather than get up at 5 a.m. and iron your bed, it made sense to prepare it the evening before and sleep on the floor with the curtains open instead. In the morning, the platoon commander, in my case a small angry Marine called Captain Bucknall, would enter the room, swipe under the windowsill with his white gloves, and without looking at the glove, thrust it in my face shouting, 'What the fuck is that!?'

'It's dust, sir!' I would reply. It wasn't my dust though. I'd wiped under there ten minutes before he came in.

'Fucking dust!' he'd scream, and with that, the irate officer would heave open the sash window, and throw the contents of my room out on to the parade ground below.

'Thank you, sir!' I would call out.

The dust probably came from the platoon commander's own house.

By the end of the first term, being shouted at was a way of life – something to be toyed with and enjoyed. If a colour sergeant is screaming blue murder in your face, the best way to fire him up a little more is to say in one's best Kenneth Williams, 'Ooh, Colour Sergeant, you're so manly!' And if, whilst on exercise in Wales, the Directing Staff have made you run up and down the same mountain three times carrying half your body weight, I'd confront them earnestly, and say, 'Colour Sergeants, if you send us up that hill one more time, I'll tell Daddy.' They would lose their shit, and send us up and down the mountain at least three times more.

Of the thirty cadets in my platoon, my best friend, Peter, was gay, which as you know, was illegal at that time in the army. He'd been to Ampleforth College, a Catholic all-boys boarding school in Yorkshire, and was open about being fiddled with by the monks there. Sandhurst was a traumatic time for him. He came out to me in his flat near the Harbour Club in London, telling me he was in love with me. I told him I loved him dearly too, but not in that way, and that my girlfriend was in the bedroom next door, and that I would be going to bed with her.

Peter's father was a hard-grafting car phone salesman from Cheshire, and when eventually, Peter came out to him too, I got a phone call.

'You've made my son gay!' Peter's father barked at me, with his mother crying in the background.

'Sir,' I said, 'I rather suspect it's a lack of love from you which might be more at fault. That or the monks.'

It made for an interesting year. We'd find ourselves back on exercise in Wales, having marched for five days straight with no sleep, and would be close to hallucinating. On the fifth day, the Directing Staff would eventually separate us into pairs. 'Buddy up!' they'd shout, and we would be given three hours to sleep, and I'd find myself in a puddle full of sheep shit under a poncho in the pouring rain with Peter prodding me in my back with a stiffy.

But Peter was my best friend for a reason. He was hysterical and ridiculous, charismatic and sometimes useless. On one inspection, Captain Bucknall stripped Peter's bedsheets, threw them out of the window, and then pointed accusatorily to a stain on his mattress.

'What's that!?' he screamed.

In a calm, almost proud voice, Peter called back at great volume, 'It's jizz, sir!'

I had been due to join the Army Air Corps and fly helicopters, like my father, but because Peter was joining The Blues & Royals, I applied to join their sister regiment, The Life Guards. Together, the regiments share bases in Windsor and Hyde Park, which is perhaps better for an aspiring musician than the Army Air Corps' bases in Germany or Yorkshire.

A few years later, Peter's younger brother, Joe, announced he was also gay. This time, I did not receive a call from his father. Joe had joined the army too, but after a night out drinking, had fallen from his second-floor room in Sandhurst on to the concrete parade ground below, breaking his back. Other members of his platoon, returning from the same bar, found him there, but thinking he had just fallen over, carried him upstairs and put him to bed. In the morning, he woke, back broken and unable to walk, and within a week was discharged from the army. Joe, like Peter, was a raging chin, with a ridiculous English accent and wonderfully flamboyant demeanour. The Americans love that, so it came as no surprise that the next time I saw him, he was in a documentary about David Hasselhoff, for whom he worked as a butler.

In 2000, the law banning homosexuality in the Armed Forces was repealed. As the senior officer present, my father, Colonel Blount, made the announcement to us from the start gate of the Downhill Race in Verbier, Switzerland.

'Listen in!' he announced. 'You'll all be pleased to hear that homosexuality is now allowed . . . but is not mandatory!'

CDT, *Take One*

In the last two weeks of my time at the Royal Military Academy Sandhurst – which was the worst year of my life – when the end was almost in sight and we were starting to practise our passing-out parade, some military police entered the lecture hall where we were gathered, told everyone to go outside on to the parade ground, and line up in three ranks.

Line by line, we were then filed into the gym, and one by one, assigned a military policeman. Each cadet was then led into the loos and ordered to pee into a beaker, with the military policeman watching as we did. On the beaker was a fish-tank-type thermometer to check that what we produced was body temperature, and not unadulterated child's urine that we'd brought in in a bottle.

Back in the gym, with the first MP still by my shoulder, a second, who was sitting behind a table, swiped my army ID card and instructed me to separate my sample into two smaller bottles. These were then sealed with a cap, and a signed and dated sticker was placed over cap and bottle, rendering it tamperproof.

For you, CDT stands for Craft, Design and Technology. For me, it stands for Compulsory Drugs Test, and Sandhurst had never been visited by the CDT team – until now.

That afternoon, I drove to my parents' house in Hampshire. It is hard to describe the panic, anguish and terrible shame I felt. I told my father what had happened that morning, and when questioned by him as to why I was so concerned, explained in a highly stressed way that some of my friends were in deep shit.

Later that evening, as I was driving back to Sandhurst, my father rang.

'You don't mean your friends, do you?' he asked.

'No, Daddy, I don't,' I replied.

'You silly boy,' he said, and hung up.

The next day, as we practised for the final parade, it felt that this was as close to the real thing as I was going to get. My eyes were full of tears as we marched. That evening, we packed our bergens and early the next morning, flew to Germany for the final ten-day exercise.

The CDT results took nine days. Throughout that time, whenever I heard anyone shout a one-syllable word like 'Fuck!', I heard 'Blount!'

On the ninth day, as I was climbing out of my sleeping bag in a forest of oak trees and bracken, Captain O'Dwyer, shouted my name. He summoned me over, and led me away from my platoon.

'I have a message from your father,' he said, and then paused. 'Your sister has passed the test for leukaemia.'

Tears began to roll down my face. He didn't know the meaning in the message. For the first time in a year of shouting, the officer's tone softened.

'If you'd told us, we would have gone softer on you. Would you like to call home?' he asked.

I was driven in an army Land Rover to a payphone on the side of a road somewhere in Germany. I didn't discuss with my father what he may or may not have done. As a colonel, any intervention would have seriously jeopardised his own career. Perhaps he had told the major in charge of the CDT that he had no choice as a father but to plead for clemency for my stupidity. Perhaps he just got the results first. Either way, we didn't discuss it on that phone call then – or ever. He simply said, 'Don't ever do that to us again.'

I went on to have a healthy career in the army, reaching the rank of captain, and then became a pop star whose USP was that I'd served in the army. Perhaps, without my father, I might just have been in *The Sun* newspaper as the first and only Sandhurst officer cadet to have failed an army drugs test. Or perhaps I was just lucky.

The Second Car Crash

Peter and I were commissioned in August 1997. I became Second Lieutenant Blount, and he a Cornet. We spent the autumn learning how to drive a tank, hide a tank, and creep around in bushes – a skill I still use to this day – and then joined the regiment in Windsor.

In December later that year, I had a housewarming party in my new flat on the Fulham Palace Road, in London. At 2 a.m., looking round and realising that I didn't recognise anyone in my house, I turned the music down and said to the fifty or so strangers, 'Would the last person out please turn off the music and close the door behind them?' And then I left for three months.

Waiting for me outside were Cornet Dan Scott and Second Lieutenant Johnny Rees-Davies in Dan's Peugeot 205 GTi. Dan drove at breakneck speed to the Channel Tunnel, and on through France. We were on our way to the army ski training in

Verbier, and had managed to squeeze three sets of skis to the left of the front passenger, between the door and the seat. At around 10 a.m., Johnny took over driving, while Dan slept in the back. I was in the front, unable to use the seatbelt because of the skis.

As we approached Avignon at ninety-five miles an hour, Johnny reached down to fiddle with the radio.

'Mind the lorry,' I said.

Johnny swerved left and immediately lost the backend of the car, as if it were trying to overtake the front. Overcompensating, he corrected to the right and we hit the side of the lorry. To give him his due, he never lifted off the throttle, and we hit the lorry at the full ninety-five miles an hour.

I tend to get quite chatty during an emergency.

'You've hit the lorry,' I informed him, as the car flipped over on its side and we started tumbling down the road.

Road, then sky, then road flashed past me in the window on my left.

'The windscreen's gone,' I observed.

'And the bonnet.'

'The engine's on fire,' I added, although I'm pretty sure both Johnny and Dan would have spotted this.

The tumbling car was beginning to slow, and the flames from the engine were getting bigger.

'Get ready,' I warned.

And then, by divine intervention, the car landed back on its wheels and came to a stop. Had it been any other way up, getting out would have been almost impossible.

'Go! Go! Go!' I shouted, as if we were debussing from an armoured vehicle.

I leapt through the missing windscreen and over the flames. Johnny didn't react, so Dan pushed the driver's seat forward, squashing Johnny against the steering wheel, and hauled himself through the driver's window on the right, and we both ran to the side of the road. The car was now substantially on fire and Johnny still wasn't moving, so we ran back, reached in to undo his seatbelt and dragged him out.

The car now completely engulfed, fuel tank and rear windscreen imploding rather than exploding with a 'whhhumpph', we stood on the side of the road, basically unharmed. The lorry driver came running towards us screaming, 'Qui est mort?'

When the fire brigade had put out the flames, the only thing recoverable were three thousand pounds in singed banknotes that Dan had brought for slush money. We hired a car and arrived in Verbier that evening with only the cash and our lives.

The Army Drugs Lecture

Ironically, every few months, the Military Police would come to Combermere Barracks in Windsor to give me, my fellow officers and the non-commissioned officers lectures on how to spot soldiers who were taking drugs. In the classroom, the officious Military Police sergeant would get a feel for the room by asking if we knew any street names for various drugs, and like children during Sex Ed, we would snigger as the various slang words were called out.

'Marijuana?' He always started with marijuana. It was his gateway drug to the rest of the lecture.

'Whacky-baccy!' someone would shout.

'Ecstasy anyone?'

'Don't mind if I do,' someone whispered.

'Disco biscuits!' called out another.

And then, getting more amped up, the military policeman would excitedly show us pictures of public loos with blood all over the walls where he claimed injecting drug users had hit an artery instead of a vein. *Amateurs*, I thought.

Towards the end of the lecture, when he was really getting a froth on, the military policeman, who obviously lived and breathed for this, asked us if we knew who the absolute worst of the worst kind of drug user was. We didn't, although in my head I was placing bets on heroin or crack.

'The lowest of the low of the drug-taking fraternity . . .' he explained in a hushed voice, '. . . is the mushroom-taker!'

!?, I thought.

'Yes! The mushroom-taker!' he exclaimed. 'For the mushroom-taker knows that after ingesting the drug, the first time he urinates, ninety-five per cent of the hallucinogen is excreted from his body – and so do you know what the mushroom-taker does? Do you!? Dooo you!? HE DRINKS HIS OWN PISS!'

Wow. I did not know that.

CDT, *Take Two*

I am not a one-hit wonder in the drug department.

And while you're reading this disapprovingly, I'd argue that the army needs risk-takers. Although possibly risk-takers who don't get caught.

Well, my second run-in with the Compulsory Drugs Test team was as a now fully commissioned officer at Combermere Barracks and not long after the Army Drugs Lecture, so I at least knew my shit. And what I can tell you is this:

Amphetamine stays in your system for up to seventy-two hours. Coke is detectable for twelve, but it's likely to have been cut with an amphetamine, so you should give it up to seventy-two hours as well. LSD and mushrooms are out of the system, as we know, pretty much as soon as you pee – and they don't test for hallucinogens anyway, so go for your life. Marijuana, however, is in your system for a week after literally just one joint, and if you're a regular smoker, up to a whole month. So steer clear. And this is if they're testing urine. If they're testing hair, you're fucked, as it's locked in the part of the hair that was growing when you took the drug. Why do you think Britney really shaved her head?

Anyway, as they do, the team turned up at the camp on a Monday morning, shut the gates, and said no one was allowed to leave until everyone had been tested.

Soldiers were ordered to the gymnasium for immediate testing, but officers could turn up when they wanted. And so, I retreated to my room in the officers' mess and set about drinking eight pints of water. Now, I'm more of a five-pint kind of guy, and downing eight pints was much tougher than I'd expected, but when I eventually peed into the beaker, the military policeman beside me looked at the perfectly clear liquid and announced, 'That's water!'

'Well, it's coming out of me,' I replied, showing him the thermometer indicating the contents were body temperature.

Back at the table in the gym, where my sample was to be sealed and labelled, the next military policeman looked at it quizzically and exclaimed, 'That's water!'

'I like to keep hydrated,' I replied, my hands shaking slightly as I separated the liquid into two samples.

Nine days later, I was summoned to the adjutant's office. I was called in, clicked my heels and saluted. Sacha Tomes, the adjutant in charge of officers' discipline, was unusually earnest.

'Anything you need to tell me?' he asked with an eyebrow raised.

'I'm wearing women's underwear?' I asked, hopefully.

'The CDT results are in,' he replied. 'Your results were "beyond clinical norms".'

'What does that mean?' I needn't have asked. It meant there was no urine in my sample. I had indeed provided them with just water.

Canada

We have, for the last thirty years, been fighting World War III on the prairies of Alberta in Canada. I know this because in 1998, soon after my second brush with the Compulsory Drugs Test team, I was sent there to fight for six months as a Russian, and the British came out and fought me. During this time, my unit and I slept out under the stars watching the Northern Lights, ran with wolves and moose, put out prairie fires, and were endlessly shadowed by clouds of mosquitoes. My unit moved, thought and fought like Russians, because if it isn't the Russians we'll be fighting in World War III, it'll be people who have bought their weapons and learnt their tactics from them. We were an effective fighting force, except perhaps Peter, who would occasionally get lost, stumble into his own soldiers in the dark and shoot them all, thinking they were the enemy.

As it was an exercise, it was considered bad form to use real bullets, so we used lasers. Each man, vehicle and aircraft had laser sensors fitted to identify if they'd been hit. So advanced was the system that it could tell if you'd been wounded or killed, or if your tank was damaged or completely destroyed – each with its own consequence on the battle. And while you sleep tonight, this battle – the biggest game of Laser Quest on the planet – is still raging.

On rare occasions, we'd sneak away to a town called Medicine Hat on the Trans-Canada Highway. Here fat truck drivers would flick Canadian loonies – one-dollar coins – on to the fannies of fat strippers. It was a sight saved for people probably on their way to hell. Towards the end of each girl's act, in between two greasy poles on a grubby red stage, the naked dancer would lie on her lower back, supporting herself on her forearms, so you could still see her breasts and face. Then, with her legs spread wide, she would grip a signed, rolled up photograph of herself between her labia. With a flick of the thumb, leering men would then toss dollar coins at her. Whoever landed their coin nearest got the poster. In the most humiliating act, the girl would then pick up all the coins around her and leave the stage. To add injury to insult, someone would eventually think it funny to heat up their coin under the table with a lighter, and then flick it on to the girl . . . and all hell would break loose.

Kosovo

The history of eastern Europe is, as you know, complicated. Over the centuries, and depending on which dictator is in play, borders are continually shifting. When one nation claims a piece of land, another argues that, at some point, it was actually theirs. Kosovo is no different. It has been fought over and claimed by Greeks, Germans, Italians, Serbs, Bulgarians, Byzantines, Albanians and Ottomans. But the fight between its ethnic Albanian and Serbian population has gone on for longer than any invading empire, and it is this fight that continues today. Kosovar Albanians see it as part of a Greater Albania, whilst the Serbs claim Kosovo as the birthplace of their nation. The two differing views cannot marry. In modern times, Kosovo was granted autonomy from Serbia by the dictator Josip Tito. By the eighties, there was a genuine push for it to become a constitutional republic. But then came the Serbian nationalist Slobodan Milošević and, with him, genocide throughout Yugoslavia. The nineties was bloody in the

Balkans, but after sitting on the sidelines watching for too long, the international community eventually decided it might be the decent thing to do to get involved and stop the killing.

And that's where I came in.

Now, if you think volunteering to be sent to war is heroic, it's worth knowing that I entirely volunteered to be sent to war in Kosovo. But by mistake.

My reasons at the time were clear – I hate Wales. I don't mean the Welsh, or the country, per se. I mean the part of Wales where the army sends us to train. It's a rocky, wet, mountainous, boggy, ankle-breaking torture zone that was chosen because it never stops raining there, and – let's be honest – other than Swindon, is the closest place in the UK to a warzone.

So, in a freezing February in 1999, there I was in Wales – again – lying in a muddy three-man reconnaissance hide that I'd dug and concealed seven wet days earlier. It's not tall enough to sit up in, so it's basically a three-man shallow grave. We had created an observation hole to the left and were positioned in a wood line, overlooking a road junction. The three of us inside had agreed a rota: observe the junction for two hours; man the radio for two hours; and rest for two hours, and this had gone on for seven miserable days and nights, with a further seven still to come. So for two weeks in deepest winter, you're buried alive with two other soldiers, observing a junction on a training area in Wales, which almost nobody ever crosses. It's pretty much hell on earth. During this time, you pee into bottles, crap into bags, and heat your food under your armpit, and that way, no one knows you're there, even if they walk over the hide itself.

In the afternoon on the seventh day, an unusual 'no play' message came through on the radio. The uncoded message simply said that D Squadron, The Blues & Royals were being extracted from the exercise and would be put on standby to go to Kosovo.

Those lucky fuckers, I thought. *Wherever Kosovo is, it's got to be better than Wales.*

And then an hour later, a gift from God. They were an officer short and needed a volunteer.

Bingo.

There was no chance anyone was *actually* going to war, and this was clearly my ticket out of there, so I grabbed the handset, called headquarters and said I was their man. I sent them my location, and as quick as an Uber, a Land Rover arrived shortly afterwards to remove me from my hide. I was beside myself with excitement. A couple of miles later, I transferred into a warm coach and giggled all the way across the Severn Bridge and back to barracks in Windsor. Once there, and with the Brecon Beacons fast becoming a distant memory, I showered, went down to the squadron roll call, climbed aboard another coach, and soon found myself on a plane to a military base in Thessaloniki, Greece, and on into what turned out to be a warzone.

Fuck.

To make matters worse, I was soon to discover that topographically and climatically, Kosovo is much like Wales. And rather than two weeks, I would be there for six months.

When we landed in Greece, on our way to Macedonia and then on to Kosovo, we were instantly attacked – by the Greeks.

Having loaded it with our tanks, we'd boarded a military train, and as we rolled out of our base in Thessaloniki, the driver, in cahoots with local activists, stopped the train in the middle of a huge crowd of waiting protesters. Armed with makeshift clubs and rocks, the protesters set about destroying the train, carriages and tanks. We were ordered to put on our helmets and body armour, and simply sit tight as they smashed up the carriages in which we sat. After they'd done their worst – a club doesn't do much damage to a tank, so it was the Greek carriages that suffered the most – the train slowly reversed back into camp.

Apparently unable to get out of the camp by train, we loaded the tanks on to low-load trucks and snuck them out the next night to Macedonia.

We set up on a training area outside the Macedonian capital, Skopje. Here we practised and prepared for war. I was a reconnaissance officer in command of a troop of fifteen soldiers and five tracked, armoured combat vehicles. Mini tanks to you. Between us, we're pretty tooled up. We've got 30mm cannon, vehicle-mounted guided missiles, handheld anti-tank missiles, 7.62mm general purpose machine guns, automatic rifles, 9mm pistols, grenades and bayonets, but most effective of all, a laser targeter, which we could use to 'paint' an enemy target for fast air to lock on to and bomb.

Any respite from training came unexpectedly. Somewhere up on a Macedonian mountain, as we were setting up a single vehicle hide and sweating in the afternoon heat, a local farmer came over carrying a two-litre bottle of 7 Up.

'Slivovitz!' he exclaimed, pointing at the bottle.

At the time, it seemed like the polite thing to do to have a drink with the farmer, and it didn't seem like a bad idea to have a second one soon after. But as dusk fell, it seemed more of a bad idea that he and I'd finished off the bottle and I could no longer see, stand up or, most importantly, locate my vehicle or my soldiers. Slivovitz, it turns out, is very strong homebrew – around 56 per cent ABV.

'How did you lose a fucking tank?' I remember asking myself, impressed at my own ineptitude. But I couldn't pronounce the answer.

'Slitheriz.'

'Slovotits.'

Either way, I'd gone from reasonably respectable army officer to tankless bum in just a few mugfuls of the stuff.

More pressingly, my squadron leader, Major Clee, was on the radio asking for my location so that he could come and check on us. Giving him the wrong coordinates was easy as I could barely see the squares on the map. Working out how to message my tank crew to ask them where they were was harder. My boss was on the same radio frequency, and the airwaves were currently full of him screaming abuse. He couldn't find us at the location I'd given him. This went on for a few hours, but in the half-light at around 5.30 a.m., long after Major Clee had given up and gone home, I found my tank – less than twenty yards away, on the other side of the bush that I was lying under.

A few days later, perhaps because my tank was so unfindably well-hidden, I was chosen by the squadron leader to take my troop up to the mountainous border with Kosovo. This was it. There was a bombing campaign in full swing, as NATO tried to crush the Serb army without direct contact. We would be working in an Italian area of responsibility (AOR) on a mission to locate and target Serb positions, as well as identify possible routes for our own assault across the border. The UK government was denying ground troops were involved in the bombing campaign.

'Don't get caught and come back with all your rounds,' Major Clee insisted. 'You're not supposed to be there.'

I saluted and turned to leave, but the major had some final words of advice. He listed the ten rules of war, some of which were as simple as, 'Be the victor, not the victim.' But the tenth was more worrying, 'Give the Italians some space – they tend to get themselves killed.'

Up on the border, it was like playing a grown-up game of hide and seek. We were looking for the Serbs and they were looking for us. Sometimes we'd find them, and we'd trained for that. Sometimes they'd find us and, to a degree, we'd trained for that too. Sometimes we'd bump into each other by mistake, and at that moment, no one really knew what to do. We'd all be really embarrassed and try to get away as if we hadn't actually seen each other.

Each morning, as it was their turf, I would tell the Italians where I wanted to go, and they would have to lead me there. I would then dismount and creep into the bushes with my recce team, while the Italians stood around and drank coffee. That said, getting to where I'd asked to go each day was easier said than done. Cross-country or along long-forgotten tracks and through steep wooded forests, the Italians were driving what looked like armoured Ford Transit vans. They'd also been issued

World War Two-era maps. This isn't unusual – standard army issue equipment is pretty much always dated and heavy. Before we deployed, I'd gone to a camping shop and, amongst other things, bought myself a green civilian sleeping bag weighing 250 grams, because the army issue one weighed in at over three kilos. I'd also bought a bit of gold dust: one of the first handheld Global Positioning Systems. Here in Kosovo, while I would be looking through the rear window of the Transit van ahead of me, watching the soldiers inside shrugging their shoulders and spinning the dated map upside down and around, I knew exactly where we were – and it was rarely the right place. Sometimes, we would be several kilometres into enemy territory, and much further than we'd planned. Trying to maintain radio silence, I would be waving, and generally failing, frantically to get their attention. Sometimes I wondered if they'd mirrored the windows on the inside.

On one mission, as we waited patiently for the lead vehicle to decide which wrong turn to take, my gunner pointed left. There were soldiers jumping out of bushes excitedly. First just a team of four, and then four more, and near them, eight more popped up like nervous meerkats.

'Serbs, sir,' said Corporal Adams, rolling his eyes slightly as if he'd just seen someone dropping litter.

I broke radio silence. Although my Italian friends in the vehicle in front didn't speak English, and I don't speak Italian, we both spoke GCSE-level French. In my case, Grade B.

'Excusez-moi,' I transmitted politely. 'Regardez à gauche,' I went on. 'Les Serbs.'

The Italian officer replied hesitantly, 'Err . . . quoi?'

There seemed to be about thirty Serbs now trying to figure out if this was the invasion, or if a tradesman in a green Ford van had simply got lost in a forest and needed help.

When confronted by a confused enemy, it's always best to look like you mean to be there and that you're happy to see them. I stood on my vehicle and waved.

'Trooper Smith,' I said to the driver through our intercom, 'feel free to overtake the Italians. Perhaps they should follow us.'

Unsure what was going on, the Serbs waved back.

The Kosovo War ended on 11th June 1999. Having bombed the enemy into submission, NATO and Serbia signed a peace accord, and the Serb army began to pull back. The same day, the Italians I had been working with drove over a mine and were blown up. Also that day, a Russian contingent of two hundred soldiers set off from Bosnia heading to the airport in Pristina. That evening B Squadron gathered together to receive our orders. My troop would be third into Kosovo, but in a humiliation for my friend Peter, he was sacked as troop leader and told to go at the back with two ambulances.

At first light on 12th June, NATO ground troops – officially for the first time – crossed the border into Kosovo. Soldiers from the Parachute Regiment, commanded by Brigadier Adrian Freer, flew in by helicopter to secure the high ground, and then an enormous column of thirty thousand soldiers began the journey to Pristina, the capital of Kosovo. Of more than ten thousand military vehicles to cross the Macedonian border that day, mine was the eleventh across.

Having secured the first five kilometres, Brigadier Freer was supposed to hand over to Brigadier Bill Rollo, who would then be in charge of the next hundred or so kilometres to Pristina. But Freer didn't want to stop. He wanted to take the glory of reaching Pristina first. The two brigadiers met at the front of the column, and overlooked by a Serbian T-64 tank, had a row. Kate Adie, the antagonistic journalist, also showed up to ratchet up the pressure, and another blond, floppy-haired, male journalist wandered over to my tank and asked what was going on.

Boris Johnson

'England need a hundred and thirty-five runs to win,' my gunner, who had been keeping an ear on BBC World Service, informed the journalist. The man, writing for *The Spectator*, credited me, the young officer, with the joke. Back then, details weren't really his thing. Some years later, he would become prime minister.

In 2006, our paths would cross again. By then, I would be the musician with the most overplayed song of the decade and enjoying a national backlash. Boris Johnson would be an MP looking for likes as much as votes. To ingratiate himself with the general public, he jumped on the bandwagon and wrote an article in *The Telegraph* describing my music as 'glutinous aspartame-flavoured schmaltz' and me as 'indescribably wet'.

My mother was incensed. So she wrote him a letter:

Dear Boris,

I am your biggest fan and supporter in Hampshire. 'Boris for Prime Minister,' I have said, with great feeling. You may not appreciate it, but at times, this has taken some arguing. What a predicament I am in now. How can I possibly continue to spread the word about what a bright, amusing man you are when you have been so wretchedly rude about my son, James Blunt? James has done well, and yet the bigger the broadsheet the greater the flack.

Jane Blount

To give him his due, four days later, Boris replied:

Dear Mrs Blount

The truth is that he is of course quite brilliant and the more I think about my outpouring the guiltier I feel. I think I kind of turned up the volume too high as I wrote. I fear it is a good old case of jealousy in the face of an intergalactic and positively orphic talent. I know that all apologies from journalists are utterly worthless but I will try at some stage to set the record straight.

With best wishes
Boris Johnson

And I guess that's his skill – he fucks you over, and then floors you with flattery, or perhaps floors you with flattery, and then fucks you over after. Either way, he's going to fuck you at some point.

I bumped into him at the Duke of Wellington's funeral – I'm married to the duke's granddaughter, obvs – and he immediately crowed, 'Blunty! How's your mother? Has she forgiven me yet?'

And at that stage, she probably had.

At the 2019 general election, Boris Johnson was elected prime minister. That evening, after the results had been announced, I went to a Christmas drinks party in Regent's Park. My wife and I had arrived early, and although it was the nicer room to be in, the upstairs sitting room was, for some reason, closed off. I guessed that our hosts would probably open up the room when there were enough guests at the party, so I grabbed Sofia and headed upstairs anyway – we might as well get in there before everyone else, I thought. But as we reached the stairs, we found ourselves being swept up with Samantha and David Cameron. The doors at the top opened, and we entered the almost deserted room. Inside were only three other people: George Osborne, the ex-chancellor, Carrie Symonds and the freshly elected Prime Minister Johnson.

'Blunty!' roared Boris. 'Look, Carrie, it's Blunty! She's a huge fan,' he said, turning back to me. None of them had slept much. As Sofia cornered the Camerons and Carrie, George, Boris and I huddled together. The gravitas of the day and the moment in the air, George and I both looked at Boris, and our new leader looked back at both of us.

'What the hell do I do now?' he asked.

Less than three years later, just as I was trying to sell my home in London, things had gone pear-shaped for Boris. His premiership was imploding, and with it, house prices collapsing. I'd already bought a new house, which at the time was the same value as the home I was selling. Suddenly, my own home was worth much less. I had also taken out a socking great bridging loan to tide me over. Now, interest rates were spiking, and the loan was costing me fifty thousand pounds every six weeks. I know, I know: Ultimate First World Problems. Now, I'm not one to pray that often, and I'm pretty certain that God doesn't normally get involved in high-end loans for the well-off, but I did turn skywards one sleepless night and say, 'Hey God. I'm a little bit fucked. Please send me a buyer soon.'

Well, amazingly, God heard my prayer, and the very next day, a man turned up and put an offer in on my house.

That man was Boris Johnson.

'Let me get this straight,' asked my wife. 'The person who is going to benefit from the vastly reduced asking price of our home is the man who's caused the crash in house prices?'

My mother was incensed. She wrote me an email: 'Don't trust that man! He's the last person I'd do business with, if I were you.'

But I didn't have a choice.

Boris texted the next day to say that he was thrilled about the house and how much he and Carrie loved it. He called me JB and I called him BJ, and we were all pally. He said he was off to Arizona to pay for it by making speeches to 'vast audiences of gastro enterologists'.

And then, six weeks later, when December had slowed the housing market to a complete standstill, and the day we were supposed to exchange contracts, Boris pulled out of the purchase.

My mother was incensed. She sent me another message: 'What an arsehole!'

Soon after that, Boris hit the news again for making his mate the head of the BBC, after he'd helped Boris secure a loan. Ethics committees were screaming nepotism, and journalists were left wondering what on earth he needed a loan of eight hundred thousand pounds for in the first place. Well, I'm sure it's a coincidence, but the deposit on my house was eight hundred thousand pounds.

Kosovo II

Back in Kosovo, the end result of the two brigadiers' argument was that Brigadier Rollo, whose command I was under, argued that Brigadier Freer couldn't lead any further, as he didn't have any armoured vehicles for protection. Brigadier Freer looked around and saw me and my five little Scimitars.

'Lieutenant,' he called over, 'get your men together. You're going to lead to Pristina.'

'I'm not actually in your brigade, sir,' I said.

'You are now,' he replied.

I radioed Major Clee and told him that I no longer worked for him, then switched radio frequencies and took my place at the front of the thirty-thousand-strong column. The paratroopers in their open-top Land Rovers took up position behind me, and some SAS soldiers in a hardtop Defender tucked in between my vehicles. Whenever we stopped, the Special Forces would open up a foldable, fabric satellite dish and relay what was going on to General Mike Jackson, NATO's commander on the ground. Kate Adie sauntered over and asked if she could sit on one of our vehicles with her camera crew, but because she's a bullet magnet, I politely declined. The Paras happily welcomed her into one of their vehicles, and we set off, the long line of armoured and soft-top vehicles stretching back further than the eye could see.

Heading in from Bosnia the day before, the Russian contingent had a head start. They aimed to reach Pristina airport before we did and claim control of the strategically important bridgehead. What had started as a controlled move into Kosovo soon became a dash to beat them there. With every booby-trapped bridge or tunnel, my new commanders were pushing us to move faster to clear them. At one such tunnel, the entranceway resembling a rubbish tip of dark green wooden boxes full of explosives, all hurriedly opened and crudely wired together, we stopped again. I was told that I should bypass it and drive through the minefield to the east. I gathered my four other vehicle commanders together and nominated one as scout vehicle, to go ahead of me. When they were blown up, another would have to pull round and take the lead. The non-commissioned officers nodded. There were no questions.

As the lead vehicle manoeuvred off the road into the minefield, a young officer from the Royal Engineers ran over from the tunnel entrance.

'It's a bit of a mess, and I can't really see what's going on, so I just cut a few wires,' he panted. 'No guarantees they were the right ones.' I didn't fancy our chances in the minefield, so holding our breath as we did, we took the tunnel.

With the mountains and tunnels behind us, the column picked up speed, past open fields and burnt-out houses. With a sense that time might not be on our side, I received a further instruction: should we get to the airport, and the Russians were there before us, we were to overrun and overpower them. I wrote the order down.

Well, around forty-five minutes later, I arrived at the airport and the Russians were already there. The Serbs had slowed us at every opportunity, while the Russians had been waved through. The order to overrun and overpower them had been received by the Paras too, and they were thrilled. Thirty thousand of us versus two hundred Russians were great odds. A Mexican standoff ensued, and what had seemed like a flippant instruction now had huge relevance, and even greater consequences if carried out. The order had come from the NATO Supreme Commander, General Wesley Clark, a man who would later run for president of the United States. But tellingly, his choice of words pre-empted his political perfidiousness. We'd normally expect to be instructed to 'engage and destroy' an enemy. He'd gone for, 'overrun and overpower', which, when you're faced with it, could mean, 'pin them to the ground and tickle them'. Several times I asked for clarification, but it never came and, to this day, I think the ambiguity was intentional.

While we were on the brink of global catastrophe, an SAS soldier quietly touched me on the shoulder and gestured to the runway in the distance. 'That isn't anything to do with you, is it?' he asked. I looked over at where he was pointing. There was a lone Scimitar like mine and two military ambulances crossing a minefield, heading directly towards the runway.

Somehow, Peter had lost a column of thirty thousand soldiers and armoured vehicles, and found himself in a clearly marked minefield on the edge of the airport. To give him some credit, he was the only NATO soldier to actually set foot on the airfield that day.

'Delta Four Zero, you should stop there,' I called over the radio. 'You're in a minefield.'

'Oh! Really!? Wow! Where is everyone?' Peter asked.

'I'm at your nine o'clock – but please don't come here. Turn round and follow your tracks back out,' I told him.

Somewhere along the way, with General Wesley Clark still pushing for us to take out the Russians, and the Paras becoming increasingly hard to control, General Mike Jackson eventually got stuck in. 'I'm not going to start the Third World War for you,' he told his superior officer, and we were instructed to pull back and surround the airport.

Two days later, the Russians wandered over, said they had no food or water, and asked if they could share ours. The NATO forces that were still there struck a deal – their food and water for an equal share of the airport . . . and with that, World War III was averted.

Closer to the Serb border, the country was a mess of burnt-out houses and death. Columns of Soviet-era T-72 tanks headed north back to Serbia. Retreating Serb soldiers were busy loading stolen trucks with TVs, fridges and sofas that they'd looted from Albanian homes. There were bodies everywhere. Old people, middle-aged men, women and children lying where they had been gunned down. Some, their skin pale and waxy, appeared to have been killed recently. Others were bloated and full of gas, implying they had died some days ago. Some, in bushes or ditches, and perhaps harder to find, were in greater states of decay, their skin more drawn and skeletal. All were accompanied by a gang of busy flies, tasting the open wounds or flitting between the mouth, eyes and nostrils.

Sometimes groups of Serb soldiers would seem surprised by our arrival, as if they hadn't been told to withdraw. They would be standing around, the bodies of the civilians they had murdered lying nearby, reading porn mags and smoking cigarettes. Only when they saw us would the realisation of guilt flash across their faces.

As we confronted them, I wouldn't introduce myself as Lieutenant Blount. Lt. Blount seemed too small. Something bigger had arrived.

'I am NATO,' I would tell them. 'You're going to fuck off now.'

At a road junction, we came across a group of fifty soldiers dug in, their weapons drawn and pointing at us. I watched them for a minute through my vehicle's gun sight, assessing their firepower.

'Don't just sit there,' Corporal of Horse McMullen warned me over the radio from his vehicle some way behind. 'You'll look weak.'

I drove to within forty metres of the junction, so as not to be enveloped, climbed out of the turret of my vehicle, jumped to the ground and walked over to the soldiers. A Serb colonel stepped out from behind some sandbags towards me.

'You should be on our side,' he said with a heavy accent. 'The Muslims are invading. We are the front line.' Then, with a menacing smile, he said he would allow us to pass through, but that he couldn't guarantee his soldiers wouldn't take it upon themselves to shoot at us as we did.

'How embarrassing for you, Colonel,' I said earnestly. 'I'm only a lieutenant, but I have complete control over my own men, including the tanks on the hillside overlooking us. You'd better tell them this – I am NATO, and if they take one shot, they will likely all die.'

The Serbs withdrew.

We entered a village that had been run as an open-air concentration camp. Thousands of people of all ages had been corralled together. The Serbs had set up machine gun posts on a hydroelectric plant on the hill above to keep watch on them, and had at times been firing indiscriminately at them for sport. Their captors no longer present, crowds of people clapped, cheered and cried with relief as we arrived, and waving children chased us as we swept along the dirt tracks.

And wherever we travelled, there were shallow graves and mass graves everywhere. Later, we would exhume them, and the living would file past in tears, trying to identify the dead from their clothing.

Sometimes, the true horror of human cruelty would reveal itself. An old woman found shot dead in her home, bound to a kitchen chair. On the table in front of her, her daughter's stripped, defiled body. Her head in a pot on the stove.

As we moved to secure the vacuum created by the Serb withdrawal, we encountered sporadic attacks by angry individuals rather than organised units. On one occasion, my troop found ourselves in a village set low in a valley around a stream and surrounded by high forest on all sides. A pair of Serb soldiers on foot were firing into the village with rocket-propelled grenades and occasional small arms fire. On higher ground in the wood line, while we were hemmed in by walls, it was hard to get a line of sight on them, so I called for air support. Now, perhaps I didn't explain clearly enough to my superiors the immediate danger we were in – I'd like to think my tone of voice was fairly business-like – but it didn't seem especially helpful of them when they offered helicopter support in forty-five minutes.

When we were sent to Kosovo, for security reasons, we'd had our mobile phones confiscated. But I'd taken three phones with me, and handed in only one. I got an electrician to install a cigarette lighter in my tank so I could charge the phones, and on top of that, I'd brought a small laptop computer and a travel printer, so that I could print off orders rather than dictate them. We already had a kettle, so all my tank was missing was a stereo. But coming under fire and being told air support wasn't coming for three-quarters of an hour seemed like a good time to use one of my phones. You'll remember my father was a colonel in the army and a helicopter pilot. Well, in fact, at that stage he was the head of the Army Air Corps and in charge of all of the UK's helicopters. So, I called Daddy.

'Helicopters?' he said, 'Yes, absolutely! Do you remember your teacher, Mr. Leakey, from Elstree?'

I did. Mr. Leakey was my English teacher at Elstree Preparatory School where you'll remember I'd been sent aged six. He was good-looking, sporty, super popular and had married the hot, blonde art teacher, Miss Sinclair, who everyone fancied.

'Well, he's a major in the Army Air Corps now, running army aviation in Kosovo,' my father explained. 'Here's his number.'

It turns out, Daddy had given Mr. Leakey a flying job when he gave up teaching, and he was about to become my saviour.

'Brilliant! Thank you, Daddy. I love you.'

'Good luck, Jimmy. I love you too.' He hung up.

It had been about fourteen years since I'd seen or spoken to Mr. Leakey, but he'd been my favourite teacher of all time and was about to become my favourite army officer. The conversation was swift and to the point. A quick description of the problem and a grid reference of where we were, and choppers were sent to my location in under five minutes.

After that, however, things started to unravel. The problem was that the helicopter pilots spoke a language I didn't – American – and there's a possibility they may have been a little charged up on something. They arrived in two Apache attack helicopters, which were an awesome sight, under the callsign 'Assassin Two-Seven', which in itself should have been a warning that shit was about to go south. As they rose up over the forest in front of us, one announced, 'Assassin Two-Seven. Armoured vehicles to our front – am engaging.'

Well, we're in the armoured vehicles, and 'engaging' means opening fire.

The sound of an Apache chain gun is incredible – but not if you're on the target end. In the ensuing melee, I scrambled on to the turret of my tank, screaming 'Stop!' over the radio, and waving a Union Jack flag over my head.

'That way, ass-fuck!' I seethed over the radio, pointing towards the forest. 'Two times infantry in the wood line to my south.'

Amazingly, we survived untouched. The forest did not. And it's anyone's guess about the two guys on foot. Tellingly, less than four years later, the Scimitars from my troop would find themselves in Iraq, and were destroyed, with a crew member killed, by two American A-10 'Tankbuster' aircraft.

After a few days, the Serb army had completely retreated back across the border into Serbia, and tensions eased. Each troop in the squadron was given an area of responsibility of around seventy-five square kilometres, where we were to police the peace. People came out of hiding and showed us where bodies, mass graves, mines or booby traps had been laid. But violence breeds more violence – Serb civilians living in Kosovo suffered violent reprisals and many fled. Empty Serb houses were looted by angry Albanians.

One afternoon, on hearing an explosion, we went to investigate and found a Kosovar Albanian begging us to come and help his friend. He led us to where his friend's body lay in the doorway of a house. He was gurgling slightly, and was also missing the left side of his face and jaw, but it was hard to be sympathetic – this was a Serb's house, and they'd planned on looting it. As he'd kicked the door open, he must have noticed the wire and pin fly past him. The grenade had been fixed at chest height on his left, and the shrapnel had left a blanket of small holes all over the open door to his right – except the perfect silhouette of a five-foot-seven human, which remained untouched – a shrapnel shadow. Not wanting to go in, we pulled him out by his ankles with his head bumping on each step.

Obviously, we're trained in first aid, so I told Trooper Smith to give him mouth to mouth. Trooper Smith threw up, so I told Corporal Adams to give him mouth to mouth.

'Sir,' he replied, 'if you can find his fucking mouth, then you can give him mouth to mouth.'

We agreed that perhaps this one was dead.

One of the issues in the country was it was awash with weapons, and the American army knows that more guns means more bloodshed, and so in a place like Kosovo, they try to remove as many weapons from the population as they can. Kind of funny that they don't apply the same logic back home. Anyway, to remove them, we had amnesties and weapons collections. However, in my area of responsibility, the Serb villages I controlled were vehemently against giving up their weapons. The Serb army had left them unprotected, and they had already suffered revenge attacks. They were very scared. But I was under pressure to remove their weapons, so we went in relatively heavy-handed. The fifty or so men of the village gathered, and I stood on the steps of a house to talk to them.

To add gravity to my otherwise childish appearance, I would take one of my most frightening soldiers, called Trooper Trencher, with me. Trooper Trencher was a six-foot-five, bare-knuckle fighter who had occasionally been promoted to lance corporal, but was always getting demoted again for violent behaviour. I'm five-foot-eight, and he would stand behind me holding a huge general-purpose machine gun – normally mounted on a tank – and after I'd finished a sentence, he would back me up by growling 'Yeah' an octave lower than me. I'd also ditched my Albanian translator, as the Serbs wouldn't have trusted either of us, and completely against normal procedures, had recruited a tall, seriously overweight Franco-Serb journalist to translate for me. Through him, I would tell the men of the village that if they gave me their weapons, I would be their friend and protect them, but if they didn't, I would be their enemy and they would face the consequences.

Cigarette in his left hand, and waving his right arm more than necessary, it struck me that my short, clear sentences seemed much longer when translated, and often caused a greater reaction than I'd expected. Eventually, after one extra long-winded translation where the crowd had all gasped dramatically and some grown men had started to cry, I asked the journalist what was going on.

'I'm embellishing your words a bit – for effect,' the obese Frenchman explained, shrugging slightly. 'I've told them that you have a Napoleon complex, and that you're a vicious bastard, and they should see what you did to the last village.'

I had assurances from my superiors that I could offer our long-term protection if the Serb civilians gave up their weapons. For them, this was deadly serious, and I looked them in the eye and gave them my word that I meant what I said. I even had two Apaches fly over the village in a show of strength.

The next day, the crowd of men of all ages nervously formed a line and handed over their guns. There were beautiful old rifles from the Second World War, Tommy Guns straight out of *Bugsy Malone*, and rusty old pistols – but nothing that an active shooter in an American high school would choose. We took photos and shook hands, and I positioned men and vehicles in and around the village.

The next day, my squadron leader radioed new instructions. We were to leave the village and given a new mission a few miles away on the Serb border. My protests were sternly rebuked. I couldn't believe it.

I called my soldiers together and told them what we were being ordered to do. They'd all seen the men of the village crying and the fear etched on their faces. They'd all heard the promises I made. So I put it to them that we would leave half the troop in the village, and the other half would move on as ordered, and that we would do this unbeknownst to our commanders. And then, unfashionably for the army, I took a vote. Everyone agreed.

For the next two weeks, my troop and I pretended to our commanders that we were all on the Serb border on a new job. With too few men in either location, we barely slept during that time. And then one morning, my boss called me. A village in Lieutenant Howard's AOR had been attacked overnight and many of the people living there had been murdered. I was to return to mine immediately.

I didn't say *fuck you* out loud – but I thought it.

'We never actually left the village, sir,' I explained. 'We promised the people there that we wouldn't, and they needed us there for their protection, so half of us stayed. We're all pretty tired now though.' When we returned to the UK, he asked me to hand over the journal that I had kept through the six-month tour, and he burnt it.

Seven years later, now a musician, I made a documentary called *Return to Kosovo*. I flew to Pristina to play a concert for both Serbs, Albanians and NATO soldiers. The next day, I took the filmmakers up to where we'd worked near the border and to my area of responsibility. The people who lived in the villages had become my friends, and I was excited to see them and capture the moment on camera. My ego had hoped for it to be a heroic moment. As we got within sight of the village across the valley, it struck me that there weren't any cars. Then, from a couple of hundred metres away, we could see that there was no glass in the windows. The wooden window frames were missing too. As we walked into the deserted houses, without furniture or carpets or cupboards, even the wiring in the walls had been removed. Only then was it clear to me what had happened – we'd promised them long-term protection. I'd handed over responsibility to some Danes, who'd handed over to some Russians, who at some point had just left. Our army had headed off to Afghanistan and Iraq. But it's anyone's guess as to what happened to the people who'd lived there.

The Queen's Life Guard

After my time in Kosovo, like Maverick in *Top Gun*, I was offered any job I wanted. So I chose the most prestigious job in the British Army – the Queen's Life Guard. This doesn't involve me sitting in red Speedos in a highchair watching the queen while she swims. Based at Hyde Park Barracks in Knightsbridge, The Queen's Life Guard is the Queen's personal bodyguard. On ceremonial occasions, we are the guys who ride beside Her Majesty wearing a red tunic, helmet and plume, steel breastplate and sword. As well as the ridiculous outfit, we'd also wear an earpiece and throat mic to communicate with armed police, and we were fully trained to protect the sovereign. We weren't allowed to stab would-be attackers with the sword as it would look bad on camera, so our job was to get ourselves and the horses between Her Majesty and the threat. We are the last line of defence. There was, however, one issue – I'd never ridden a horse before.

So they sent me to the Army Riding School in Melton Mowbray, Leicestershire, for four months prior to getting the job. There, with Peter on the same course, we were put on rejected, unrideable horses that bit, kicked, bucked and rolled, for four hours a day. A week in and I had blisters the size of fifty-pence pieces on each buttock. If you fell off the horse, you were put straight back on – sometimes even if you were still unconscious. One officer was even lifted back on his horse after he'd fractured his spine. But by the end, you could ride anything.

Throughout the time there, we were assigned our own horse to fall off, and like every army course, attention to detail was the mantra we lived and died by. After mucking out the stables, even the piles of horseshit would be inspected. In the army, kit is 'squared away', but shit is 'squared off'. Squaring your horse's shit off into perfect, inspectable square piles of poo is an arduous task. We would drive Captain Birkbeck's flat-backed Peugeot 309 round to the stables and reverse it at speed into the shit to save time. And if you lost your temper with anyone on the course, your threat to them was always, 'I'm gonna fuck your shit up.'

For royal protection, we trained on the runways of decommissioned airfields in Suffolk. A horse-drawn carriage would be produced, and Peter would be thrilled.

'I'll be the Queen!' he would announce.

Then young soldiers dressed in helmets and body armour would try to attack the carriage with an array of weapons and slogans, while we charged them down on enormous Cavalry Blacks. Whilst many of the young soldiers were hospitalised, Peter, you'll be happy to hear, remained untouched.

After all that, we qualified, and I was posted to London.

Now, it's quite a thing finding yourself on parade next to the Queen for the first time. I was positioned by the rear left wheel of her carriage. There were a million people lining the streets, and millions more watching on television at home. There's a lot to take on board: four reins in your left hand; a sword in your right; a monarch's life in both. The horse is steered as much with your legs as your hand. The helmet is kept secure with a chainmail strap under your bottom lip. Your left thumb triggers the microphone. But the horse I was on had done the job many more times than me, and as we rode down The Mall, I was feeling the first glimmers of confidence and soaking up the crowd. Then, at some point around halfway along, the horse went about twelve inches too far forward of the carriage wheel – and that's when my new boss introduced herself.

'*Will you get back!*' she said sharply. 'They've not come here to see *you*.'

The horse and I looked at each other, terrified, trying to work out which one of us she was talking to.

Now based in London, I lived with my sister, Emily, in a tiny, two-bedroom flat above a drycleaner's on the Fulham Palace Road. It's a busy street and people on the top deck of London's double-decker buses could look straight in through the window, into our sitting room. But it had its benefits. There was a zebra crossing directly outside the front door, which led perfectly to the entrance of a Sainsbury's Local opposite. There, we could stock up on booze. A Boots beside the drycleaner's was where we would obtain hangover cures, and the drycleaner's itself was good for the clothes we had been sick on. My mate Billy, who was broke, lived on the sofa in the sitting room. Our kitchen sink looked on to our neighbours' kitchen sink, separated only by the two panes of glass and a metre of air between us. Although we didn't know the neighbours, we'd often wash up at the same time and wave to each other, sometimes comparing washing up liquid as we did. Our tiny loo window looked on to their bedroom, which didn't have curtains or a lampshade, and our neighbours had a curious habit of leaving the light on whilst having aggressive sex. Billy would occasionally wake my sister and lead her to the cupboard-sized room where our loo was.

'Look at that,' he'd say, pointing through the window at the neighbours, excitedly.

'Oh my God!' she'd reply.

They'd watch for a moment, and then become uncomfortable and return to their beds.

Billy wasn't paying any rent but would rack up various bills along the way, and eventually I thought it might be time to find him somewhere else to doss down. I'd befriended a seventy-year-old gay man, called Ed, in a club in Chelsea, who kept trying it on. I told him I wasn't into it, but that I had a good-looking but impoverished friend in his late twenties who needed a home and would be willing to pay in kind, rather than in cash. Billy moved into Ed's spare room the next week – although I failed to tell Billy the precise details of the deal.

On the first night at about 10 p.m., Billy called me from his bedroom, where he'd had to barricade himself in.

'You promised him WHAT?' he shouted.

Ed texted me to ask what was wrong. I told him that Billy probably needed a little warming up.

That weekend, I went to visit to see how things were going. Ed had gone away for the weekend to his house in the country, and Billy needed lunch and a conflab. I arrived at around eleven and rang the bell, unknowingly catching Billy in the shower. As he didn't answer, I began walking away, and moments later, Billy opened the door wearing only the tiniest of handtowels. Realising I'd walked off, he ran out on to the street and called after me.

'Hey, Blunty!' he called.

As he did, the front door shut behind him.

'No?' he said disbelievingly. 'No! No!'

There was a window open on the first floor, so Billy started shimmying up the drainpipe – hand towel concealing less and less the higher he got. A crowd gathered to watch, assuming this was Ed's new young lover, and he lost the towel about halfway up to great cheers.

Paul Simon and Brian Eno

My girlfriend at the time lived in Notting Hill with her parents, Tchaik Chassay and Melissa North. Tchaik and Melissa had co-founded the Groucho Club and often hosted eclectic parties, to which I was occasionally invited. At one, I found myself having dinner with the musician Paul Simon, producer Brian Eno and only five other people. For me, this was extraordinary – not only were they the first people I'd ever met in the music business, but they were my absolute musical heroes. I have all of Paul Simon's music and am a diehard fan of Eno, who produced some of U2's best work. But the bubble burst when the two decided to have an ego-off.

Waving one hand in the air like the queen, Paul announced that he was a genius and had done everything one could do in music. Brian cut in to say he was also a genius and was even more remarkable as he had invented a whole new genre of music.

I am not a genius, so I kept quiet.

The others round the table were all thoroughly enjoying the explosion of immodesty, and as the smash and return of egos went on, the other dinner guests convinced the two musicians that if they were both genii, they should work together and make an album.

And they did – in Primrose Hill Studios, where they fought like six-year-olds and ended up falling out. Eno, in the end, was not credited as producer, and the album was called *Surprise*, which, perhaps unsurprisingly, no one has heard of. They did give me a free copy though.

Company of Gentlemen

While I was the Queen's ceremonial bodyguard in London, I set up an escort agency. The idea was relatively simple – I'd provide young Household Cavalry officers to escort rich American women round London, be it to restaurants, theatres or drinks parties. It wasn't meant to be about sex, per se. But in the end, it didn't really pan out that way.

I got a dedicated mobile phone, and using an online web design program, built and launched a website called 'Company of Gentlemen'. It was pretty rudimentary, and business never really kicked off, except for a handful of calls asking if I'd have sex with the caller's wife while they watched.

I needed to up my game. But making a slick-looking website cost money I didn't have. This was the era of Friends Reunited and A Small World, which ran on HTML code, so I taught myself some basic computer coding, and started looking around at various websites for inspiration. Along the way, I came across

99

Quintessentially, a global luxury concierge service. At that stage in my life, I hadn't been in many hotels, and the word concierge sounded pretty much like a French word for escort. The company was founded by Ben Elliot, who went on to be co-chairman of the Conservative Party, which again, makes me think escorts. But most importantly, Quintessentially's website looked really professional. I copied the site's HTML code on to my computer, swapped their logo for mine, changed some of their photos for others I'd downloaded from the web, and added some text explaining what we at Company of Gentlemen did.

Bingo. The phone started ringing off the hook.

I went on the first job myself, just so I could say that I had, but after that I had a roster of captains and subalterns that I'd send out from Hyde Park Barracks. We charged three hundred pounds a night, of which I kept a hundred for myself. We all kept fairly tight-lipped about what we were doing, and it was great business. But for a serving officer in The Life Guards, it was also very scary. When I was on duty, I'd give the company phone to my sister, Emily, who ran a personal assistance business and was especially good at fielding calls.

We had about six months of plain sailing, but one evening, I returned to my flat on the Fulham Palace Road and found Emily there looking distressed. She'd had a call from Quintessentially's lawyers, she explained. They planned to sue for breach of copyright and defamation of brand.

Time started to move slowly as the adrenaline kicked in. The computer took forever to turn on and my hands were shaking as it did. It took half an hour to delete the Company of Gentlemen website and remove any trace of Quintessentially's code from my computer. When you logged on to www.companyofgentlemen. com, you were redirected to a new site called www.verysorrysir. com. The page simply read, 'We at companyofgentlemen.com are verysorrysir.com if we have in anyway upset, affected, breached or defamed anyone, in this life or the next. Amen.'

The lawyers didn't call back.

CDT, *Take Three*

Yeah, there was a Take Three. While I was at Melton Mowbray. So, like I said, when the CDT team arrive at a barracks, they close the gates and no one leaves – and by that, I mean nobody. No matter how senior you are, or which doctor's appointment you need to get to, everyone gets tested, and only then can you think about leaving. They turn up at random, although usually around once every three months, and probably on a Monday. Thinking about it, pretty much anyone with any brains could probably predict when they would come next.

Well, there we were, riding round the indoor riding school at Melton Mowbray at 8 a.m. on a Monday morning. The outdoor *manège* was being used for a showjumping competition – some brigadiers and colonels had flown in from as far afield as Germany to compete – so we were stuck indoors and being shouted at by a corporal major. And then an announcement came over the Tannoy.

'All personnel are to return to the accommodation blocks. No one is to leave camp. Return directly to the accommodation blocks immediately.'

I didn't even know they had a Tannoy.

Still sitting on our horses, everyone turned to look at each other. Someone asked if perhaps there'd been a fight the night before – but I already knew what was going on.

'CDT,' I said out loud.

Back in my room, I set out on a now well-trodden path. I drank as much water as my little body could take. Eight pints in, bladder bulging so much that it was painful to walk, I made my way to the gym. But as I did, I was met by the strangest of sights. Instead of the orderly queue that should have been outside the temporary test site, there was a herd of senior officers in jodhpurs and No.2 Dress jackets braying outside. Getting within earshot, it became apparent that they were furious. The most senior brigadier was dressing down a sergeant from the Military Police.

'It's a disgrace! This completely disrupts our riding competition!' he was saying. 'How dare you just turn up like this!'

'It's designed to be a surprise, sir,' the MP explained.

'We will not comply!' the brigadier fumed.

'The C does stand for compulsory, sir,' the sergeant explained, pointing to the CDT team badge on his lapel.

In the end, however, after a barrage of abuse, the military policeman relented.

'It is against Standing Orders, sir. But at your insistence, those of you in the riding competition are excused the test. I will, however, be raising this with my superiors.'

'Do that!' the brigadier replied angrily. 'Let's go!' he told the crowd of officers. 'Oh, and thinking about it . . . we'll need to take one other person to announce the riders and horses, and to record the scores.'

Ever my saviour, Peter chirped up, 'Captain Blount is especially good with a microphone, sir!'

'Captain Blount? Your father's dog isn't called Doris, is she? She is? Oh, perfect. Come with us!' And with that, I was extracted from the CDT team's clutches.

I spent the rest of the day in a portacabin overlooking the outdoor *manège*, desperately trying to announce the arrival of 'Colonel Farquhar, riding Passchendaele' in a normal voice while kneeling on the floor and trying to pee out of a crack in the door without being noticed.

Todd Interland

We kept two hundred horses at Knightsbridge, riding them around the streets of London at 6 a.m. each morning, past nightclubs I'd fallen out of an hour before. If we weren't on duty, the evenings were our own. One night, I went to my first ever gig. It was at a tiny venue called The Water Rats in King's Cross, with a capacity of only two hundred – and bizarrely, I was the singer that night. My friend Billy and I had invited about a hundred and fifty girls from Chelsea along. It was a bit of a dive, so the girls all sat on the floor on their pashminas, and Billy passed round some pre-rolled joints to try to get them into the music.

And that was how it started. I played shitty bars and clubs to between five and fifty people for two years. All the labels came to listen – but none of them signed me. Then in June 2002, a man called Todd Interland phoned me out of the blue. He was Elton John's junior manager and he'd just listened to 'Goodbye

My Lover' on a demo CD in his car, he explained. We arranged to meet at the Electric on Portobello Road, and within a week he was my manager. We've been together ever since. That same week, I marched into Colonel Ridley's office at Hyde Park Barracks, saluted, handed him the same demo CD, and told him I was resigning to become a pop star. He told me I was an idiot – but he could have been referring to any number of things.

My final job in the army was to stand by the corner of the Queen Mother's coffin as she lay in state in Westminster Hall for three days. People queued up for twelve hours to file silently past, as we stood, heads bowed in her honour. It's a weird moment. You're dressed in all this hot, heavy gear – helmet, armour, sword and plume – and all you can see is people's feet filing past. There's a huge sense of history but, in reality, all you're trying to do is not pass out.

The next day, I marched behind the coffin in the funeral procession, and after that, Captain Blount was no more.

EMI Music Publishing

In the music industry, there are two kinds of deal. There's a record deal, where you're signed as the recording artist, or singer, and there's a publishing deal, where you sign away the rights to your songs as a songwriter. Recording artists also break down into two categories – there are rock stars, which is what I wanted to be, and there are pop stars, which is what I ended up being.

Well, while I was looking for a record deal, and wanting to be a singer, EMI Music Publishing heard my demos and offered me a publishing deal for my songwriting. It wasn't huge – a two hundred thousand pound advance for a five-album deal. That's basically a £200k non-recoupable loan, which I could potentially use to help me secure a record deal. Todd thought it was worth taking, so we went to sign the deal.

Apparently, the oldest you should admit to being in the music industry is twenty-five. I was twenty-eight. So, when the lawyers put the paperwork down on a low table in front of me, with Todd looking on in horror, I signed the contract, putting my year of birth as 1977 instead of 1974. If you cross a 7 halfway down, it looks pretty similar to a 4, so I had a get-out clause, but with that, I defrauded my first contract.

Ever since, I've been editing my own Wikipedia page to say that I was born in 1977, although annoyingly, as she doesn't know it's me doing it, my mother goes on Wikipedia and changes it back.

Anyway, paperwork signed and cheque in my wallet, I climbed on my motorbike and drove home to my tiny flat on the Fulham Palace Road, passing Hyde Park Barracks as I did. Outside, I spotted Trooper Trencher guarding the main gate, SA80 rifle in hand. I pulled over.

'Hello, sir!' he exclaimed enthusiastically. 'How's life in the music business?'

'Well, now you mention it,' I said, pulling out the cheque, 'take a fucking look at this!'

'Fuckin' 'ell!' he said.

And then from his combat trouser pocket he produced a newspaper cutting. It was a *Daily Mail* article about the longest ever recorded sniper kill – 2,475 metres – with a large picture of Trencher above it.

'Never thought I'd be famous before ya, did ya?' he said, smiling.

I really didn't – and especially not for killing someone.

A few weeks later, having heard I'd signed a deal, my friend Jonny Blenkin got in touch to suggest we buy a house together in Belgravia as an investment. As a builder, he would organise the renovation and rental. Why not? I thought, and chucked in some cash. And although I'd never seen it, for a while it was quite cool to say to people that I owned a house in Belgravia.

I didn't actually think about the house for a few years, until one day I called Jonny, mainly to complain that the rent on the house was crap and that I'd love to take a look at it, to see what we could do to improve it.

'Cool,' he said. 'When's your flight?'

'I'm in London already,' I told him.

'Yeah, but when's your flight to Bulgaria?' he replied.

It turns out, I didn't own a house in Belgravia after all.

EMI Records

When I was nineteen years old, the same Jonny dropped a demo tape of mine through the letterbox of a man he knew was in the music industry. The man, Neil Ferris, was CEO of a label called Ferret & Spanner, and amazingly, he called and offered me a deal. Excitedly, I travelled to London and, without an appointment, walked into the offices of Russell's music lawyers on Great Portland Street and presented them the deal I had been offered. They charged me two hundred and fifty pounds for their advice, and in those five minutes, explained that the deal – a five-thousand-pound loan in return for all my music publishing, past, present and future – was the worst deal they had ever seen. Subsequently, Russell's are still my lawyers to this day, and I didn't sign the deal with Ferret & Spanner.

Two years later, I turned on the television and saw a young band who had just been signed to EMI Records by an A&R man called Raz Gold. I made a note of the A&R man's name and wrote him a letter pretending to be my friend Jonny. Although Jonny was a builder, I didn't say that. I just wrote saying it had been great to meet Raz the week before, and I was excited for him to meet the young artist I had told him about called James Blunt. At the bottom, I signed 'Jonny Blenkin' and put my parents' phone number.

The next Monday, my mother shouted up to me in my bedroom, 'There's a man on the phone who wants to speak to your friend Jonny. He says he's from EMI!'

By Thursday, I was in the EMI offices in Brook Green, in west London.

You're thinking this is how I got my big break – but it didn't turn out that way. When I turned up, I was led up to Raz's office. I played him half a song on my guitar, and then he cut me off excitedly, and said, 'You've got to listen to this, man!'

He turned to his stereo, hit play on the tape recorder, and on came some dub-style music. Over it, a man's voice started saying, 'I'm walking down the street, and I'm trippin' off my feet, and all that's on my brain is – cocaine!'

Raz Gold didn't offer me a deal.

Two years after that, and now an army officer, by coincidence or fate, I was introduced to a young man called Dan Ferris – son of Neil, from Ferret & Spanner. His father was now head of EMI Records and Dan took me to see him. We recorded some demos at the EMI offices, and everyone there, including both Ferrises, got very excited. 'You're going to be a star!' Ferris senior told me.

Recording session over, they all came to watch me depart. I had a 1200cc silver Moto Guzzi motorbike, and in my leather jacket, for a moment at least, I looked cool. I slung my guitar over my back – bearing in mind this was the guitar that I'd strapped to the outside of my tank in Kosovo and had survived the warzone – saluted them goodbye, revved the engine, and at one and a half miles an hour, fell over, smashing the mirror, indicator – and the guitar.

The bike was too heavy to lift on my own, so they all had to help. They laughed as they did, and although I was laughing with them, on the inside, I was crying.

I drove off, and when I got round the corner, I got off the bike and stood there, calling myself a prick for a few minutes.

EMI Records didn't offer me a deal.

Virgin Records

In the search for a record deal, I got turned down by B-Unique Records, Big Brother Records, Columbia, Decca, Demolition Records, Island Records, London Records, Parlophone, Polydor, Relentless, Silvertone, Sony Music (I might have fluffed that meeting as I turned up on a horse in full ceremonial gear), Universal Music, V2 Records and many more.

Eventually, however, Todd got a call from Virgin Records saying they'd heard my demos and been to a couple of gigs and they wanted to sign me. This was the first serious offer I'd had, so not only did Todd come along, but the senior manager from the management firm, Derek McKillop, came too. Derek is an old-school, sweary manager with a broad Scottish accent, and was personally managing Elton at the time. Like many Scots, he didn't beat around the bush and was a good person to have onside in a fight.

The boss of Virgin, Philippe Ascoli, was a bit of a legend in the industry. He had signed cool French bands like Air and MC Solaar and was just signing KT Tunstall, so we were excited about potentially working with him.

We got a cab up to Kensal Road, and there were quite a few people in the Virgin offices waiting for us. There was a sense of excitement on both sides, and everyone couldn't have been more effusive. They introduced themselves, and said what they all did, and then took it in turns to say, 'We love you. You're going to be a star.'

And then the marketing director, Steve Morton, who is married to the DJ Jo Whiley, perked up and said, 'We love your music, but we do have one issue . . . with your speaking voice. Any chance you can do a different accent?'

I paused for thought, and then replied, 'I can do Pakistani?'

Derek, a man with a strong accent himself, stood up and barked, 'Let's get the fuck out of here.'

We didn't sign a deal with Virgin Records.

Custard Records

With the remaining money from the EMI publishing deal, I flew out to Austin, Texas, to play at the South by Southwest music festival. By now, I'd been rejected by every UK record label, and this felt like my very last shot. I'd convinced two musicians to come with me, and any excitement dissipated when we saw that rather than play at the main festival, we had been booked to play on the top floor of the Crowne Plaza Hotel on the outskirts of town to a crowd of twenty people. It's hard to think of a less inspiring place than a top floor lobby of a cheap hotel, and it seemed like a long way to have travelled to play to just a handful of people, but it was a thirty-minute gig that changed my life.

As I finished and put my guitar down, a five-foot-two, leather-clad, heavily tattooed woman came striding over in huge platforms that made her almost normal height.

'I'll give you a cheque for quarter of a million dollars right now if you'll sign with me tomorrow!' she said.

'Deal,' I replied.

We went out and got drunk and she gave me a cheque. The next day her lawyers sent over the paperwork, and that's how I got signed to Custard Records.

Linda Perry

The woman I'd signed to in Texas turned out to be Linda Perry, lead singer from the band 4 Non Blondes – so she's a one-hit wonder too. And that's not the only similarity. We're both afflicted with a lack of height and we've both suffered prejudice, in that she's gay, and I'm posh.

I was the first artist to sign to Custard Records, an independent, Los Angeles-based label. It was also her first foray into being a record label boss, and we got on like a house on fire. When the dust had settled on the signing and South by Southwest, I flew from London to LA. Waiting to meet me at the airport were three black limousines, Linda Perry herself, and an entourage of nine lesbians.

I sat in the back of Linda's limo for the forty-five minute journey to West Hollywood. Once there, we drank tequila shots on the rainbow-flagged strip on Santa Monica Boulevard, and as the bars closed, they took me to Cheetahs Strip Club.

As we entered the building, everyone stopped to watch this unimpressive little English guy walking in with no less than five girls on each arm. At the table, Linda summoned over a bunch of strippers, and assigned me the nine-months pregnant one.

By 2 a.m., full of tequila, we piled into the cars and drove back to Linda's. The girls took all their clothes off, jumped into the pool, and started making out with each other. I looked skyward, mouthed, 'Thank you,' took off my clothes and jumped into the water.

Now maybe it was the cold, or it could have been the pressure of the moment, but it quickly became apparent that what I had wasn't impressing anyone. I swam up and down past the naked, kissing, grinding, moaning, heavenly throng, meekly saying, 'Anything for me? Anything for me?'

There was nothing for me.

Carrie Fisher

One Sunday, Tchaik and Melissa invited me to join them for lunch in a restaurant called 192 in Notting Hill. The actress Carrie Fisher was there, and she asked me what I did. I told her I'd just left the army and was moving to Los Angeles to record an album.

'Where are you gonna live?' she asked.

'I haven't organised anything yet,' I replied.

'Then you're gonna live with me,' she told me.

And I did.

She became my best friend. I was with her the night before she died. She was godmother to my eldest son and the only person we let visit the hospital when he was born. She arrived smoking a vape, drinking a Diet Coke, with twenty-five shopping bags and a balloon. Later, she had a cigarette in the loo. And she came to our house in London to say goodbye before getting on the plane on which she would die. She'd just scored two 8-balls of blow – one for her, and one for her dog Gary, who was also an addict.

I moved into Carrie's house in September 2003. I'd arrived carrying two bottles of champagne, and as there was a group of people in the house having some kind of party, I waved them both enthusiastically in the air, till someone pointed out the banner over the door saying, 'Congratulations Hailey – ONE YEAR CLEAN!'

Carrie put me up in Cabin No.2 and flicked the switch on the neon sign above the cabin entrance from 'Vacancy' to 'No Vacancy'.

Her mother, the actress Debbie Reynolds, also lived on the property, in a smaller bungalow below my cabin. Debbie was famous for movies like *Singin' in the Rain* and *How the West Was Won*, and together Carrie and Debbie were considered Hollywood royalty.

Most mornings at around 11 a.m., Debbie would shout up at me on my wooden terrace, 'Hey Charlie! You want a drink?'

I'd shout down, 'Morning, Debbie. I'm James.'

She'd shout back, 'You sure you're not Charlie?'

'Pretty sure,' I'd reply. 'I'm James. I've been here for a couple of months now.'

After some thought, she would shout up again, 'You wanna drink anyway?'

The Charlie she was referring to was my roommate, Charlie Wessler. Charlie was a movie producer who lived in Cabin No.1. He'd made films like *There's Something About Mary* and *Dumb and Dumber*, and he shared his cabin with Gort, the dog that starred in *There's Something About Mary*. Gort had been trained to do tricks like shake your hand and jump out of windows – but you had to be fairly careful with that one. Charlie also owned a stuffed dummy version of Gort that they'd used in the movie. People would come round to the house for dinner, and Charlie would introduce them to Gort. Then later, he'd hide Gort away, and ask the guest to go and grab the ice cream from the freezer where, unbeknownst to them, he'd have put the fake Gort. They'd find the frozen Gort and start screaming, and we'd all find it pretty funny.

Carrie lived on a bend in the road on Coldwater Canyon in Beverly Hills, and the house was a sight. There were chandeliers in the trees, ceramic bees in the garden and fairy lights every-where. Inside the Mexican hacienda-style house, skies had been painted on the ceilings, a heavily decorated Christmas tree stayed up all year, and a million weird things lay everywhere. She was a collector of memories. Every surface had an object, and every object had a story. As I left my cabin to play the piano that played itself in her bathroom, I would pass a cardboard cut-out of Carrie dressed in the *Stars Wars* bikini outfit, on which she had written her date of birth and date of death on the terrace outside my room, a British telephone box in the garden and C-3PO in lingerie on the porch. It was like living in an acid trip.

That said, for the first few weeks, I didn't see much of Carrie or Charlie. I'd head to the studio soon after my morning interaction with Debbie and arrive back late at night. Occasionally, I'd go to the kitchen in the house to get some tuna from the fridge. The kitchen was normally empty of people by the time I got there, but after about a month of living there, I opened the screen door to find the eighty-year-old African American cook, Gloria, and the Mexican handyman, Michael, in a troubled conversation about Carrie. They were concerned for her mental well-being and were discussing calling a doctor.

'She's not making any sense,' Gloria was saying.

'Has she taken her medication? Michael asked.

The weird thing about this whole conversation was that Carrie was in the room with them.

Carrie was bipolar, or manic depressive, and occasionally had manic moments. During those moments, most people thought she was mad. But if you concentrated really hard, you could see that she was just connecting the dots faster than everyone else, and they just weren't keeping up. Instead of going from A to B, she was jumping straight to F. It turns out, being a manic depressive is a bit like being on LSD – which explains the house. And as a guy who will happily skip out letters in the alphabet, I suddenly felt right at home.

'I get it,' I told her.

'Come with me,' Carrie told me and led me to her bedroom, where we sat and talked till dawn.

From that day on, when I got back from the studio, instead of going to my cabin, I'd go straight to her room. She'd be there, scribbling away on a pad of yellow paper, and I'd sit at the end of her bed, and we'd watch old movies, and talk about war and Hollywood.

It felt very much like a home. In my earliest days there, I wrote a song called 'You're Beautiful', recorded another called 'Goodbye My Lover' in her bathroom, and together, we named my first album *Back to Bedlam*, because of the madhouse from which it came.

But Charlie and I weren't the only house guests. Different people would come and go. Carrie had been married to Paul Simon, so his son Harper often came to visit. Sean Lennon would store guitars there. In the day, anyone from Meryl Streep to Courtney Love to Joni Mitchell might pass through, all congregating in Carrie's bedroom. One afternoon, Carrie's brother, Todd, came to visit for the first time since I was staying there. He'd brought his wife and son, and later on, they decided to stay the night. What with them, Carrie, Debbie, Debbie's helper, Carrie's daughter Billie, Charlie, Michael, Gloria and me, it was a full house.

I'd been out that evening, and in a first for me, I brought someone back to my cabin. She was an Austrian who I'd known for a couple of weeks. Now, as I'm sure you've imagined, I'm a pretty quiet lover, but her being Austrian, and as it turned out, really loud, it sounded pretty much like a German porn movie in my room. I had her up on the basin in the bathroom, and she was screaming, 'Ja! Ja! Oh ja! Ficken mir! Oh ja! Das is gut. Schneller! Ficken mir! In das poopie!' I carried her into the bedroom and threw her on the bed, and she landed on the TV remote, so I pulled it from under her and whacked it on the bedside table, and we carried on, and, for the sake of the story, I'd say about fifteen minutes in, I suddenly looked over at the bedside table and saw all the lights on the intercom were on for all the rooms in the entire house – and realised that I'd hit it on with the TV remote.

I reached over and pressed the button to switch the intercom off, and we froze. The girl looked at me and after a pause said, 'Ve carry on?'

And then, a solitary light flashed back on on the intercom, beside the label that said, 'Carrie Bedroom', and Carrie's voice sang out through the speaker saying, 'So what happened ne-eeeext?'

In many ways, it's hard to explain the relationship. I was closer to Carrie than almost anyone else in the world, except my wife. She told me which girlfriends weren't suitable, was the first person I told when I met my wife, and we chose engagement rings for her together. She also knew where every unmarked grave of mine lay and where every guilt stemmed from. She was complicit too. When I arrived home one morning with a blue-black love bite on my neck, and my girlfriend of the moment about to arrive, Carrie grabbed her sixteen-year-old daughter and gave her a love bite as well. Then Carrie summoned me over, offering her own neck, and told me to give her a love bite. When the girlfriend arrived, we all had love bites.

In 2007, I was nominated for five Grammys, and you'd think that I'd have won at least one of them, so the night before the ceremony, Carrie wrote my acceptance speech. This was what was on the piece of paper in my pocket that night, and what I would have read out if I'd won:

Thank you. Oh, thank you! I can hardly sing. I feel so horny. And this award – it's so Yul Brenner. Oh, thank you again. I just want everyone to read in the tabloids that even in my wildest fits of self-loathing, I never would have made daddy promise that this could ever validate my own mediocrity. And to the other suck-ass nominees, I want each of you to know how totally wonderful your fake smiles make me feel right now! You know when they first told me I was not the father, I just had to take a

Xanax and obsess about how great my thighs have been. I guess it all just makes me feel kind of cheap. You know, there are so many star-fucking, Napoleon complex-suffering label execs to thank! First off though, I want to rim the self-congratulatory circle-jerks of the Grammys, who looked deep within their Magic 8-Balls before giving me this fantastic award! Also, I want to thank Charlton Heston for being such a powerful force in my life. And to the hooker with the heart of gold, who taught me to take life by the balls. And finally, to all the groupies I slept with – I couldn't have done it without you! THANK YOU, AMERICA, AND GOODNIGHT!

I didn't win, which on the basis of the speech alone, is a shame. As it was, the Dixie Chicks won my Grammys. They had been vilified by everyone the year before for their anti-Iraq War stance, but by 2007 the court of public opinion had changed, and they were suddenly the darlings of the music scene. Even though they didn't have an album out, they still won Album, Single, Video, Dance Routine and Haircut of the Year. But I'm not bitter.

When Carrie died in December 2016, she'd been flying high, back on the silver screen as Princess Leia – the character that had made her famous. But it had come at a price. She was acutely aware that while men are allowed to grow old, in her business, women are not. She had also been under pressure from the producers of *Star Wars* to lose weight. In an attempt to do so, she'd switched the medication that treated her bipolar disorder, and as a result, had a manic episode on the first day of filming. The producers, who'd taken a gamble reviving her character, panicked. The shame with which she spoke about this afterwards was heart-breaking.

There was also an issue with drugs. Carrie had long been open about her addiction, but at some point, it was obvious enough to be of concern. Friends of mine called to say they'd seen her being carried off a plane unconscious. She took uppers by day, and downers on flights. And at night too. I stood many times at the foot of her bed at 3 a.m. listening to the laboured breathing of someone sounding close to death on heavy medication. I asked her to be godmother to my son, telling her specifically that I wanted her to take care of herself so that he might know her when he grew up. Charlie, her best friend, confronted her more directly and told her she needed to quit, but was ostracised by her as a result. I took a different approach and did them with her, pretending to myself that I would guide her to redemption one day – just not today. The lies we tell ourselves are the hardest to forgive. As a result, her daughter Billie blames me in part for her death, and no longer speaks to me.

At the time, I'd assumed it was cocaine that would take her, but I was wrong. As the flight taking her home to Los Angeles was coming in to land, they hadn't been able to rouse her. The opiates she'd taken as she boarded had supressed her body's urge to breathe, and she had effectively been suffocating for much of the flight. It took her a couple of days to die in that Beverly Hills hospital that all the famous people die in. As my family and I got to France to celebrate Christmas, my manager texted me, simply saying, 'Sorry to hear about Carrie, James.' I called the hospital to tell them what she'd been taking, but the toxicologist had already identified the makings of a pretty serious party.

Carrie would say that her mother Debbie was always trying to get in on her act. Well, sure enough, the day after Carrie died, Debbie went and died too. Some people said she'd died of a broken heart. I think Debbie just saw an in, and held her breath till she expired. Either way, they had a joint funeral, which would have pissed Carrie off no end. Debbie went down in a regular casket, but as were her wishes, they buried Carrie's ashes in a giant ceramic Prozac pill. You can see a picture of it on the CD disc of my first album. There are only two of them in the world, and the other one is my most treasured possession.

In pretty much the same sentence, Carrie also said she was worried that her brother would probably fight with her daughter over her house and estate when she died. Well, after Carrie's death, her brother Todd auctioned off the contents of her house – but before he did, he first filled it with extra things that I'd never seen in the house before and that looked like they'd been acquired at a Star Wars convention. Billie bought back some of the genuine things from the house at the auction, including the piano that lived in the bathroom. At the same time, I'd heard rumours that tickets were being sold to the funeral, and so when Todd offered to fly me there by private jet, I couldn't work out if it was a really kind gesture, or if it was to boost the numbers of celebrities there. Either way, although it killed me, I didn't go. At the service, Todd played a song of mine called 'Courtney's Song', telling the press that I'd written it specifically for Carrie – but there's a clue in the title.

In May 2023, Carrie was given a star on the Hollywood Boulevard. Billie oversaw the guest list, but didn't invite Todd, and they both gave interviews briefing against each other.

After Carrie died, I was homeless in Los Angeles. I moved to the hotel in which my band used to stay – Le Park Suites, on Melrose. There, there were still stains on the floor that I remember making some ten years earlier, and the ghosts of afterparties I can't relive. Just like that, I felt lost in a city I'd called home. And so, one morning, I decided I should swing by Carrie's house. I didn't know if anyone would be in, but I needed to go back to feel something of her. The studio I was working in was sort of on the way, and although I mentally tussled with myself at the traffic light on Sunset Boulevard, in the end, the desire was too great, and I turned right on to Coldwater Canyon. I drove up the hill to the bend in the road about halfway up, turned right into the driveway and stopped, facing Carrie's arched wooden gate. On it, half a dozen painted metal signs still read things like 'Beware of crabs' and 'No swimsuits in lobby'. I got out of my hire car, walked up to the gate, and put my hand on it.

'God, I miss you, Carrie,' I said, and for the first time since her death, tears filled my eyes and rolled down my face. I really miss her so much.

At that moment, two open-topped Star Map vans, that go round Hollywood showing tourists where celebrities live, pulled up and stopped. And over the Tannoy, the tour guide said, 'If you look here on your left, you'll see the late, great Carrie Fisher's house – and as you can see, some fans are still deeply moved by her passing.'

Tom Rothrock

My producer was a man called Tom Rothrock. He'd recorded super cool people like Beck, Elliott Smith, Badly Drawn Boy, the Foo Fighters, and then me – which, as he pointed out afterwards, was when all the cool kids stopped calling him. I'd got in touch with him because I loved his production on the Elliott Smith albums, and bizarrely, the night before I called, he'd stumbled across my live performance of 'You're Beautiful' from South by Southwest online – so it was meant to be.

The journey to find him hadn't been easy. Linda Perry had wanted me to work with Bill Bottrell, who'd produced Sheryl Crow's *Tuesday Night Music Club* in 1993. But when I met Bill, there was a sadness in his eyes. In the years after the Sheryl Crow hit, he and his wife had decided LA was too dangerous to raise their family and had headed up north. They'd bought a house on a cliff overlooking the sea, but then things went tragically south. Playing in the garden, Bill's son fell off the cliff and died. Soon after, a girl called Shelby Lynne, whose record he was producing, ran off with his wife.

'I need this to be a hit,' he'd told me, which seemed the wrong way round.

Coincidentally, that weekend I'd been at Shelby Lynne's birthday party in a suite in the Chateau Marmont hotel. As I'd opened the door to see a group of about forty girls cheering on Shelby and a stripper, who were on the floor wrestling each other in their underwear, they all stopped and looked at me in disgust, till Linda barged past me shouting, 'Don't worry – he's with me!'

Linda had also introduced me to Vincent Gallo, who'd made the movie *Buffalo '66*. He spent the whole meeting trying to pull Linda, and at some point, she had to pull the plug and we left.

So, finding Tom was a moment. He looks like American Jesus – if Jesus was into skateboarding and motorbikes – and instead of turning water into wine, he turns my whine into something palatable. Each morning at 11 a.m., I'd leave Carrie's and drive to Tom's, taking Mulholland Drive, along the very top of the Hollywood Hills. On my left, the square grid of The Valley stretched out all the way to a mountain range in the distance. On my right, West Hollywood, Sunset Boulevard and Santa Monica Boulevard. Cross the 105 Freeway, and Tom's house was up by the reservoir, in sight of the Hollywood sign. At 11 p.m. each night, we'd have a drink, and on the journey home, I'd stop my car and look out at the city twinkling below.

When it came to recording 'Goodbye My Lover', Tom didn't have a decent piano, so as the sun set, we decided to head to Carrie's, as she had Paul Simon's old piano in her bathroom.

I wanted to get deep in on the song, so I'd bought a hash brownie from a hippie in Topanga Canyon. I told Tom my plan, adding that as he's my producer, I needed him to get high too. Tom is a considered man, so he said I should eat it first, and he'd see how I was doing – and then maybe he'd join in. The hippie had said the brownie was super strong and strongly advised only eating a quarter – but it's an important song, so I took a half. Anyway, we packed up our gear to head to Carrie's, and bang on the forty-five minute mark, it hit me. And fuck, did it hit me. I was so high I wanted to tear my own skin off. I could hear two people having an argument with each other and both of them were me.

Tom walked in to see how I was doing.

'It's pretty mild,' I told him.

He took a half too. Then we drove over to Carrie's house, and as we arrived, that's when Tom came up.

'Take me to hospital! Take me to hospital now!' he started screaming.

Slightly panicked, I found that if I played the piano, he would calm down. So, I played the song, and the engineer recorded, and Tom sort of shook a bit, and we both tried to ignore the brown terracotta walls that were definitely breathing beside us. But at the end of each take, I'd stop playing and he'd start screaming again.

'Yarrrrgh! Fuck, it's too much! Take me to hospital! Please!' he'd shout.

Trying to get to a hospital was out of the question, so when the engineer felt we had enough piano takes, I switched to recording the vocal. Tom had taken his cowboy boots off and was groaning in a leather chair in the corner, and it struck me that I was pretty baked too. As I sang the song, it occurred to me that maybe this is it? You get the deal, you record the song, and then you die. And I sang that song like it was my last, and as I got to the last word . . . I passed out.

At that moment, Carrie started banging on the bathroom door shouting, 'You want any soup!?'

And because the music had stopped, Tom jumped up and screamed, 'TAKE ME TO FUCKING HOSPITAL!'

And the engineer stood up and shouted, 'What the fuck is wrong with you people?' and left.

But we had it in the can – and that's what's on the record.

Elizabeth Taylor

Carrie walked into my room one afternoon and asked me if I'd like to meet Elizabeth Taylor.

'Fuck yes,' I replied.

Carrie's father was the pop star, Eddie Fisher. He married Carrie's mother, Debbie Reynolds, but later ran off with Elizabeth Taylor, which is about as big a deal as when Brad left Jen for Angelina. Anyway, Eddie's dead now, and it's all water under the bridge, and Carrie's daughter was round at Liz's house, playing with Liz's grandson and needed picking up.

So, we drove out to Liz's place in Belair. I didn't see much of the house. There was a pool and some security guards, and if you put your hand out to touch one of her Oscars or BAFTAs on the shelf in the sitting room, an infrared beam triggered an alarm and one of the security guards would run in and say, 'Step away from the awards, sir.'

Carrie called me over to the bottom of the stairs, pointed up and said, 'Hey James, meet Liz. Liz, meet James.'

I looked up and there Elizabeth Taylor was, and she looked down at me from the top of the stairs and said, 'Hey James, I can't come down – I've got the shits.'

Ashton Kutcher and Demi Moore

One night, I was invited by two English producer friends of mine to Ashton Kutcher and Demi Moore's house in Beverly Hills for dinner. There were some other people coming too, like Natalie Portman and her Navy SEAL boyfriend, making up a group of about twenty in total. They were all pretty safe, conversation was fairly grown up, and no one got drunk. Except me.

After dinner, we moved to the sitting room to play a game called Werewolves. Ashton explained the rules: each person is given a card, which only they see, telling them if they are a villager or a werewolf. The idea is that werewolves 'kill off' villagers and the villagers try to 'kill off' werewolves. Whichever group is completely killed off first, loses. The game has a moderator, who tells you all that it's night-time, and everyone closes their eyes to 'sleep'. Werewolves are then told to open their eyes, identify each other, and silently choose one villager to kill off. They then close their eyes again, and the moderator announces that morning has broken, and everyone can open their eyes, at the same time discovering which villager has been killed by the werewolves and is out of the game. From here, the whole group tries to reach consensus as to who amongst them might be a werewolf. The group must then delegate one person to be killed. As they die, that person reveals their card to show if they were a villager or a werewolf. And so, this game of attrition goes on each 'night' and 'day' until one group wins. There's no physical indication if someone is a werewolf or a villager – you just accuse each other and look for their reaction. The game gets pretty heated. Ashton Kutcher is quite loud anyway, and you're only working on how people respond to accusation, and the best way to do that is to put them under some pressure.

There's also a twist. A Romeo and a Juliet card are handed out. The two recipients are made aware who the other is. If one of them is killed off, the other will automatically die – so they will try to protect the other at all costs.

Well, along the loud, shouty, accusatory way, while everyone is hurling this obscenity and that, trying to force a blush or stumble out of each other, I notice that Natalie Portman's Navy SEAL boyfriend is sticking up for another guy way too much whenever he's accused of being a werewolf. Through the melee and heckling and wine, it was clear to me what's going on.

'I've got it!' I shouted, jumping up and pointing at the butch Navy SEAL. 'He's Romeo – but Juliet's a fucking man!' I said, pointing to the man he was over-defending, 'So Romeo is gay – and Juliet's a werewolf!'

Everybody stopped and looked at me.

'What did you say . . . ?' someone asked.

'These two!' I exclaimed. 'They're Romeo and Juliet, except – ha! – it's Romeo – Romeo. You see?' I said, limping my wrist as I did. 'And he's a werewolf!'

Now what I hadn't taken into account is that while my generation of Brits have grown up watching *Carry On* movies and Benny Hill, the Americans – especially the Californians – hadn't. What I thought was sarcasm and childish innuendo looked to them like a shit sandwich. And worse, it turned out the Navy SEAL, whom I thought was Natalie Portman's boyfriend, was actually gay.

'So what if I'm gay?' he said.

'Same rules apply!' I explained.

'I mean it,' said the Navy SEAL.

'That's great,' I said, 'but not really my point. He's a werewolf, and you're Romeo and he's Romeo too, or whatever you like to call him . . .'

There was a protracted silence.

'Listen,' I said, searching for a defence. 'My best friend is gay!'

I had found a hole and a shovel and I was using it.

'Guys, honestly. I went to an all-boys boarding school. I joined the army to be around men. I'm almost an honorary gay!'

The game ended. Ashton Kutcher asked me to leave. My English producer friends were asked to leave too.

We walked out on to the sidewalk and under a streetlight, they both looked at me.

'What the fuck did you just do?' they said.

It was a rhetorical question.

Michael Jackson

I arrived back from the studio one day and walked into Carrie's bedroom to find her there with the producer Quincy Jones. I wasn't sure of the context, but as I came in, he was saying, 'We've been telling him for years – "Michael, stop fuckin' the kids!"'

Michael Jackson was still alive at the time, and although he'd been to court, he wasn't convicted of anything. Carrie had a load of badges made up saying, 'I slept with Michael Jackson', which she made us wear.

David Kitt

I had signed to a tiny independent record label called Custard Records, but to achieve worldwide distribution, Custard licensed me to a major label called Elektra. Well, just as I finished recording my first album, Elektra collapsed. But from the ashes of Elektra and another insolvent label, East West Records, rose Atlantic Records. Of the seventy-seven acts on Elektra's roster, Atlantic ditched seventy of them, and kept only seven. Now, as I had just recorded my debut album, I was naively confident that they would keep me on, but my manager Todd explained that it doesn't work like that. My album had only cost about two hundred thousand dollars, and that would be considered a tiny write-off compared to their investment in other acts. As it was, the label had decided on six artists they were going to keep, but the seventh was a choice between me and an Irish musician called David Kitt.

So, Atlantic Records set up a gig at Bush Hall on the Uxbridge

Road in London. David Kitt would headline, and I'd be the support act, they said. Effectively, whoever did best on the night got the deal. We tried to treat it like a normal gig, and as I was the support act, contacted Kitt's team to discuss logistics. His management said I could use his sound man, so I didn't need to hire one, and that we could share the dressing room.

Back then, I didn't have a band, so I turned up with a bearded keyboard player, called Beardy, and my sister Emily, who was going to shake an egg and do backing vocals. When we arrived, Kitt and his band were already sound checking, so we hung around and listened. He had a full band, and they sounded tight. His songs were good too. But then, rather than stopping and giving us the stage to sound check at some point, they sound checked right up until doors opened and the public were let in, denying me the chance to check my own instruments and sound. At that point, they also told me that I couldn't use their sound man.

With the public already in the hall, we set up the guitar and keyboard. The venue's own sound woman was kind and asked if she could help, and if she should do either our monitors or the front-of-house. I asked if she'd do front-of-house, as that's what the audience and record label hear. Emily had never done a gig before, so she wouldn't have known if the monitors were turned on anyway.

We stepped backstage to gather ourselves, and I walked into the dressing room to change T-shirts, with just a few minutes before we went on stage. There on a sofa was David Kitt. We hadn't yet met or spoken.

He looked up at me and said, 'Ah, James Cunt.'

I looked back at him and replied, 'Ah-ha, David Shit.'

Anyway, I played, then he played, and I got the deal, and I've been on Atlantic Records since 2004.

'You're Beautiful'

Okay, we should probably talk about that song now.

I wrote the lyrics to 'You're Beautiful' in Hyde Park Barracks in under two minutes. It was 2002, and I'd just walked past my ex-girlfriend and her new boyfriend – who I didn't know existed – at High Street Kensington Underground Station. She and I caught eyes, and although it felt like we lived a lifetime in that moment, we didn't react, and I went back to the barracks and wrote the words. Admittedly, the lyrics were a little different at first, and went as follows:

> These drugs are brilliant.
> These drugs are pure.
> I saw an angel.
> Of that I'm sure.

Which explains why I went on to say, 'She could see from my face that I was fucking high.'

Everyone thinks it's a saccharine-sweet, romantic song, but it's actually about a guy who's fucked up on drugs, stalking his ex. Weirder still, it went on to be the UK's most-played song at weddings, when the last line is, 'I will never be with you.'

A few months after the ex-girlfriend Underground sighting, I flew to Los Angeles to write with a friend called Sacha Skarbek. As Sacha and I were heading to his house in Beechwood Canyon from the airport, he stopped to get a coffee, leaving me in the car listening to the radio. And as I sat there on my own, the DJ put on a song called 'La Cienega Just Smiled' by Ryan Adams and dawn broke in my mind. Instantly, I started singing the lyrics and melody to 'You're Beautiful' over the top of his song.

Between them, these two moments changed my life.

Back at the house, with Sacha at the piano, me at the guitar and Ryan's four chords in our pockets, we finished the song. As we were fine tuning, his housemate, Amanda Ghost, walked through the room. I was singing the song to Sacha, and Amanda – unsolicited – made a passing comment about it needing a bit more work to tie up the end of the chorus.

'I'm not sure the end makes sense,' she said, followed by the words, 'By the way, I'd never take anything from you for that kind of advice.'

It seemed an ominous thing to say.

A couple of weeks later, through her lawyer, Amanda demanded 10 per cent of the song. I called Sacha, who was also the keyboard player in her band, but he said he didn't want to get in a fight with her, in case she gave him the boot. Without Sacha, Todd advised we give her the 10 per cent rather than get into a legal dispute. Against my better judgement, we did, and soon after, she fired Sacha anyway.

When I went on to record the song with Tom Rothrock, I had another, slightly smaller issue. Custard Records said I had to change the words 'fucking high' for something less explicit. It was a heated debate, and Linda Perry was insistent that the song wouldn't sell or be heard as it was.

'But how high do you think I was?' I asked.

In the end, I sent them a new version of the song with the lyric: 'She could see from my face that I was particularly high', and at that point, they gave up.

We put my debut album out in September 2004, with a single called 'High', which got me my first bit of airplay on the radio. Then we put out a song called 'Wisemen', and the album jumped into the top twenty in the album charts. And then, on 18th May 2005, we put out 'You're Beautiful' and by 17th July, the world had changed. I was in a hotel in Locarno in Switzerland, about to support Jamiroquai, when the record label's radio plugger called to say that, after six weeks in the UK charts, the song had climbed to number one and my album had knocked Coldplay off the top spot too. The news was terrifying. I hung up the phone and paced up and down the room, swearing. The song was such a monster that after four weeks, we tried to stop it being number one any more, by limiting CD production and delaying CD delivery. We failed, and after the song was played to death at radio, there came the big backlash, and I became a national pariah.

And that was my music career.

Anyway, I'll never have a song that big ever again, which is probably a blessing for all of us. And as my Twitter bio says, one song is all you need. But the weirdest thing about having a global megahit is how people disparage it, as if it's something to be ashamed of. I get called a one-hit wonder by none-hit wonders, and they always ask me in interviews if I'm sick of playing the song, but I'm really not, I love it – I'm just sick of the question.

In other events, after the song hit, Amanda Ghost would go on to do interviews saying she wrote the song – implying she'd written the whole thing. Jay-Z even phoned her, demanding to write with 'the girl who'd written "You're Beautiful".' Arguably, she made a career out of the claim, talking her way to heading Epic Records for a brief but reportedly disastrous twenty-month spell. The *Hollywood Reporter*'s article about her was entitled, 'Who Destroyed Epic Records'. And for me, it didn't end there. Having been given an inch, she then demanded 15 per cent of my song 'Wisemen', bizarrely claiming she'd written the chorus. I'd written the song seven years before she and I had met, and this time, I had an ace up my sleeve – back in 1995, when I wrote the song, I'd sent a demo of it to myself by recorded delivery. Yeah, I'm one of those guys who actually did that. Anyway, we got an independent musicologist to study my demo and the recorded master, and his conclusion was comprehensive – she hadn't written it. Amanda wouldn't accept the professional's findings, so I jokingly offered to let her use a non-independent musicologist, hired exclusively by her, who she could pay to prove her point, because no matter which way you spin it, he wouldn't have been able to. The pre-trial meeting quickly started to become farcical. Eventually her manager turned to her and said they should leave, and Amanda was hauled off still screaming that she'd written a song in 2002 that was on a tape from 1995.

I have been in the business for over twenty years, and so I should be over it, but some things are not worth forgetting. Still to this day, I get calls from people saying that Amanda Ghost is trying to fuck them over. Amy Wadge, who co-wrote Ed Sheeran's 'Thinking Out Loud' was the most recent. FKA Twigs before her. We may soon have enough to start a Victims of Amanda Ghost group.

NRJ Music Awards

With 'You're Beautiful' now all over the radio in Europe too, I was invited to perform in Cannes at the NRJ Music Awards. These are the French equivalent of the MTV Awards, and so basically irrelevant – unless you win one. It's the same for The Brits by the way. Americans might describe them as 'provincial'. Anyway, my girlfriend and I were staying on the seventh floor of the Martinez Hotel, overlooking La Croisette. This was the hot hotel to stay at, and where the official afterparty was held. At the ceremony, I won the award for Best Newcomer, and we celebrated back at the hotel, although celebrating anything with Bob Geldof is like dragging a tapeworm out of its host body.

At around 3 a.m., we called it a night and went to bed – but at some point, I woke up to hear a footstep in the room. In the darkness, I felt for my girlfriend. She was still there beside me and, judging by the snoring, still asleep. I heard a second footstep and wondered if I was allowed to wake my girlfriend up and ask her to deal with the issue, or whether I had to deal with this myself. By the third footstep, I was up, naked and screaming like a bitch. A man of normal height – a couple of inches taller than me – stood there in the darkness. Momentarily, the thief was paralysed by what he saw – a naked man-boy making a sound similar to a terrified rabbit. Looking for a weapon, the first thing I saw was the heavy, gold-coated NRJ award that I'd left on the bedside table. I picked it up and swung it at his head, connecting with more precision than I had expected. He reeled backwards, and for a moment, I was emboldened, screaming and swinging the award at him furiously. He ran through the open balcony door and then, to my horror, leapt off the balcony.

Still naked, I ran to the balcony railings and peered over. I expected to see a body seven floors below on the pavement. And then I saw the scaffolding that the little fucker had climbed up, and on which he was now swinging down, like a monkey, to make his escape.

'Come on, motherfucker!' I called to him, waving the award, as the sun broke gently over the Croisette.

I called reception and told them to get security outside as fast as possible to catch him.

'But are you okay, Monsieur Blunt?' they asked.

'Yes, absolutely,' I replied.

'Bien,' they replied. 'Et bien dormir,' as the thief ran off along the Croisette.

The next day, I was performing on a French TV show in Paris called *Star Academy*. Alone in my dressing room, there was a knock at the door, and a French record label rep popped his head round the corner.

'Would you like to say 'ello to Lionel Richie? 'E is asking for you.'

'Definitement,' I said, which means definitely.

The man led me down the corridor till we reached a door with an A4 paper sign taped to it saying 'Lionel Richie'. He knocked and without waiting for a reply, opened the door and let me in. Television dressing rooms all look pretty much the same and contain the same seven items of furniture. This room was no different. A foldaway grey plastic table with stackable plastic chair in the far-right corner carried some warm soft drinks. A white faux leather three-piece suite with a low table in front, on which there were some bland-looking crisps in a bowl, was the focal point of the room. A hanging rail to the left stood empty. And, as always, some cheap white venetian blinds blocked out any natural light from the unopenable windows, so the strip lighting above made it more of an interrogation room than a place you'd want to wait all day before you sing your new three-minute song.

Lionel Richie was on the sofa, dressed in black, and immaculately groomed. His tightly trimmed beard looked almost painted on. And in the corner by the table, a tall, fat Frenchman stood, with what looked like a hot, blonde trophy wife.

Lionel stood up warmly and without introduction said, 'You know James, when I wrote "Hello", God was in the room with me, and he said, "Hello? Is it me you're looking for?"'

'When I wrote "You're Beautiful",' I told him, 'I was as high as a kite on drugs, and was trying to pull someone else's girlfriend.'

Lionel nodded.

149

'That's beautiful,' he replied.

And then the Frenchman stepped in, handing me a business card as he did, and gestured towards the woman next to him saying, 'If you want one of these, call me.'

Larry David

From that moment on, life got pretty weird. Elton John would call to check in occasionally, and I'd hear myself saying things like, 'Hold on, Elt – Mick Fleetwood's on the other line.'

I also started getting invitations to extraordinary events. I was asked to play at a celebrity skiing weekend in Deer Valley. There I got to race with Lindsey Vonn and other world-class skiers. Afterwards, I was whisked into a VIP tent for a drink, past someone who was desperately trying to talk their way in, but having no joy.

'I'm a fucking celebrity, man!' the man was insisting to the large bouncer on the door.

It was Larry David – from *Curb Your Enthusiasm*. He's basically just the same character in real life.

That evening, I gave an acoustic concert for the event, and afterwards, all these famous people were swept into my dressing room to say how fantastic I was. It was quite a moment – Robert

F. Kennedy, Glenn Close, Gwen Stefani, Neil Patrick Harris and Pat Monahan from the band Train, to name a few, standing there looking at me, all saying how wonderful I was, and as they did so, I found myself gently and continually being pushed out of the way by some guy who was just helping himself to, and eating, my food in my dressing room.

It was Larry David.

Ahmet Ertegun

In June 2006, there was a story in the papers about a five-year old girl who'd fallen from a balcony, fracturing her skull and leaving her in a coma. She was unresponsive for ten days until her favourite song, 'You're Beautiful', came on the radio and she suddenly woke up. Never mind the doctors who had fought night and day to keep her alive – I was credited with saving her.

In October of that year, Ahmet Ertegun, the founding father of Atlantic Records and revered record label boss, tripped over at the Beacon Theatre in New York during a Rolling Stones concert. Devastatingly, he struck his head on the concrete floor and fell into a coma. The news spread quickly, and soon after, I got a phone call from the executives of Atlantic Records saying I needed to get on a plane from Ibiza and head to New York immediately. They were adamant that if I would just sing him the song, he would come round.

'Guys, I'm not Jesus,' I said and didn't go.

Ahmet died the next day and the executives at Atlantic have never really forgiven me.

Seriously though, what if everyone who was sick suddenly started calling?

If I'm honest though, I've actually started getting used to it. I was at a party the other day where a French woman in her fifties with wild blonde hair and a leopard-print onesie grabbed me overexcitedly.

'C'est lui!' she kept exclaiming at me.

I speak a bit of the lingo, so nodded at the right times as she told me her story. Her daughter had cancer of the ears and couldn't hear, she explained, till they played her two of my songs, and she got her hearing back. Amazing. I gave her a hug and thanked her for telling me. She was obviously mad, but it's a sweet story. I wandered off and, perhaps a little cockily, told my wife, Sofia.

Later, Sofia, who is half-Belgian and fluent in French, bumped into the same woman. The woman excitedly relayed the same story with a couple of details that I'd missed. She's a massive fan, and all she'd ever wanted to do is meet me, so tonight was a big deal for her, and last year she'd taken her daughter, who has cancer of the ears, to my concert in Paris, but after two songs her daughter's ears hurt so much that they'd had to leave.

Sofia came to find me with a smirk on her face.

Bobble

After 'You're Beautiful' went big, I went on tour forever. At least that's how it felt. I packed up my flat on the Fulham Palace Road, sold Emily on eBay, and never really came back.

Realising I was leaving, my dealer, Ted Gant, who ran Raffles nightclub at the time, asked if he could move into my empty flat. I'd already arranged renters, but he was insistent he wanted it and would pay. He begged me to cancel the renters, which I eventually did, and gave him the keys.

Three months later, Ted still hadn't paid any rent. I called Emily from my tour bus. That afternoon, she brought her car round to the flat, and with the exception of his plasma TV, which she sold, she piled Ted's belongings into the boot and then drove round to Raffles. There, she unceremoniously dumped everything on the doorstep. That same day, Ted was caught doing dodgy deals with the club's money and was fired, and his girlfriend, who worked on the door, caught him shagging another member of staff and dumped him. Evicted, fired and dumped in a day.

I was three months into a world tour that would last two and a half years, and from then on, I was pushing out around two hundred and sixty concerts a year. To this day, my tour still consists of two tour buses and five trucks, with sixteen people sleeping on each bus in coffin-sized bunks. We're a team of around forty people in total. I generally play arenas, which are bigger than theatres but smaller than stadiums.

My tour manager's name is Robert Hayden, but we call him Bobble. He was given the moniker by The Libertines, who he tour-managed before me. They were, by all accounts, a trickier bunch to manage than me. On our bus, if there's a spare bunk, we call it a 'junk bunk', to dump stuff like wash kits, guitars and stuff. On the Libertines' – a band with a taste for heroin – the 'junk bunk' was used for something entirely different. Our bus drivers tell us a terrible story about the lead singer of another band with a similar habit who got a groupie onto the bus, injected her with heroin – she'd never done drugs before – and when she subsequently overdosed, they apparently dumped her on a beach, called an ambulance, and left the scene.

Anyway, Bobble also tour-managed Simply Red, The Flaming Lips, Placebo, oh, and the *Walking With Dinosaurs* tour.

When I started working with him, Robert was a twenty-four stone, ginger, sweaty, fully functioning drink and drug addict. He's also up there on the spectrum. He remembers every fact and figure on any subject. You can ask him how many tickets we sold in Berlin in 2007 or what was the name of the girl that Karl, the drummer, pulled in Oslo in 2005, and he'll know.

'Thirteen thousand, four hundred and thirty-nine, and her name was Agnes,' he'll say knowingly.

He also has some quirks – he is socially uncomfortable, has never shaken someone's hand whilst maintaining eye contact, and is generally happiest when things are going wrong. He has a strong suspicion that society is about to collapse and everything is the UK government's fault, even if we're in a different country. But he runs our tour as effectively as the best sergeant-major, and cares for us all as if he were our mother and we his children. He is the guy who writes 'Belfast' at the top of my setlist, because the last time we performed there, I'd told the audience how great it was to be in Dublin. He is also the most accident-prone human being on the planet.

He once broke his arm while I was on TV – he was alone in my dressing room – by falling over a clothes rail. He apparently leant on it, but it was on wheels, and I returned to find paramedics escorting him out. When the arm healed, it was slightly crooked, so at an angle, but two degrees less than the amount legally required to claim benefits.

In Sacramento in 2006, Bobble was having breakfast on his own on the terrace of a busy restaurant, when a female homeless person stopped on the street opposite to watch. She shouted loudly and incoherently at the customers for a few minutes, and then pulled open her beige velour tracksuit bottoms at the front, put her hand deep inside them, shat into her own hand, and threw the shit at the restaurant. It landed on Bobble.

In 2009, because of his size, a doctor told Bobble that he was borderline diabetic and was on course for an early death. In that instant, Bobble gave up drinking – because that's where the calories are. At the same time, he kept up the drugs – because that's where they are lost. He also adopted a strict routine of daily, hour-long angry marches, normally along the side of very busy roads. This all happened when we weren't on tour, and I hadn't seen him for about a year. Then, when we were about to go on the road again, we agreed to meet at the Cumberland Hotel by Marble Arch to catch up. As I waited for him in reception, I saw a man walking towards me whom I didn't recognise, but for the familiar gait. It was Bobble. To my disbelief, in the year since I had seen him, he had lost a full twelve stone and was literally half the man he was before.

To celebrate this achievement, the band and I took Bobble out for dinner, and for the first time in a year, he drank – cider – and in the process got very, very, very drunk. So drunk, in fact, that when he got back to the hotel, he fell asleep in his clothes and threw up so much in the bed that his BlackBerry drowned in his vomit.

In the morning, a maid from the hotel knocked on the door.

'Help me,' he asked. Together they stripped the bed, the maid's head shaking.

The BlackBerry could not be resuscitated.

That afternoon, all of us with hangovers, we met Bobble for a curry, and on the Underground on the way back to the Cumberland, as the curry reached his intestines and he started to sweat, Bobble realised that this had been a bad idea. Skipping uncomfortably out of the carriage, along the street and through reception, he made it to the lift. Thirty painful seconds later, the lift doors opened, and he scuttled along the corridor to his door, opened it hurriedly, pushed into the bathroom, pulled down his trousers, spun his bottom towards the lavatory, but failed to make it to the loo, and shat liquid all over the floor.

As he did, the doorbell rang, and the same maid he'd met that morning called through the door, 'Turndown service?'

He opened the door saying, 'Help me.'

The maid poked her head round the bathroom door and recoiled in horror.

'What the fuck is wrong with you!?' she asked.

Crowd Surfing

From the earliest days of touring, I became a prolific crowd-surfer. It just goes with the territory with my kind of music. But it has been a journey. The first time I crowd-surfed was in Barcelona. I'd invited a ton of friends along to the show, and halfway through a song, I ran and jumped, and in mid-air watched as the crowd underneath me parted like Moses and the Red Sea. I managed to get a fingertip to the seventh row, who were slower to move than the first six, and this fortunately stopped my chin impacting too hard on the floor.

What a prick, the audience thought.

In the Aragon Ballroom in Chicago, in order to reach the audience, I jumped down from what must have been a ten-foot stage, in the hope of then mounting the barrier and launching myself on to the crowd. As I landed, however, the enormous security guard in the pit couldn't figure out who the hell I was. He pounced on me, pinning me to the ground. Trapped beneath him, I was screaming, 'I'm the singer! I'm the singer!' till some other security men peeled him off and let me go.

In Asheville, North Carolina, I jumped off stage and ran down the aisle, high-fiving as I went. I got as far back as the sound desk, but when I tried to break right, my brand-new leather-soled shoes offered no grip. I slipped and fell hard. Picking myself up, I fought my way through the crowd to the stage, took up my position at the piano, and as I hit the next chord, heard myself play the wrong note. Looking at my hand, I realised my finger was pointing in the wrong direction.

At the end of the song, my guitar technician came over to hand me a guitar.

'Brian,' I said, 'I think I've broken my finger.'

And in a broad Glaswegian accent, he replied, 'Well, you've got nine others.'

After the show, and in hindsight, rather stupidly, rather than consulting a doctor about my finger, I decided to ask my drummer, Karl Brazil, what he thought. Karl's real name is Gary Pratworth, but he changed it to Karl Brazil when he first took up the drums. Anyway, he assured me that if I could bend it, the finger wasn't broken, and so for ten more weeks I played on, with what has now become a fairly misshapen implement. When I did eventually see a medical practitioner in New Zealand, rather than show great interest in the finger, he was more interested as to why I might seek advice from a drummer on any given subject.

I've played at Glastonbury three times – twice on the main Pyramid Stage. The last time I played was to an audience of eighty thousand, just before Amy Winehouse and Jay-Z. Halfway through, I dropped down off the stage, and crowd-surfed over the huge throng of people, and for a moment there, I was cool.

On my return to the stage though, my heart sank. The stage was too high for me to climb back on to. Panicking, I looked up and saw a man I didn't recognise looking down at me.

'Help me!' I pleaded. 'Please help me!'

And then I noticed the large camera on his shoulder, and realised he was the BBC TV cameraman, broadcasting live to the nation, and that I was basically begging the nation for help – thus cementing my position as the least cool person in the business.

Glastonbury has always been my favourite place to play, and the memories I have are mostly not about music. My first time there, when a friend lost their phone and asked me to call it, someone in a Bristolian accent answered, simply saying, 'I've got your mate's phone – and I'm keepin' it!' before hanging up.

My second time, at 7 a.m. and having not yet gone to bed, my half-Indian friend Nin and I sat in the Love Fields on the 'L' of the twenty-foot-high 'LOVE' sign, watching the sun come up. Below us, an unconscious female marshal in a yellow hi-vis vest lay face down and motionless. After a couple of hours, she slowly roused. With grass and leaves still stuck to her face, and a strong West Country accent, she looked at Nin, then pointed at me and shouted, 'N*gger lover!' Then she pulled her trousers down and peed into her knickers, before pulling the soggy ensemble back up and collapsing face down in the mud again.

My third Glastonbury, I came off the Pyramid Stage, and with Elvis shades and a leather hoodie, went back up to the same Fields of Love selling laughing gas to passers-by. As they would inhale the balloon, and the gas take hold, they'd eventually get a proper look at my face, and as they started asking the question, I'd say, 'Yep . . . That's two pounds.'

The Golden Ticket

I know you'd expect a James Blunt tour to be fairly sedate, so it's hard for me to tell you about it without sounding like I'm either lying or bragging. Perhaps the easiest way to understand it is like this: there are five of us in my band, and three of my bandmates married girls from the audience.

How they met is what I'm going to tell you about next, but put simply, they weren't the first girls from the audience that my bandmates met.

On the road, we'd play a concert to a few thousand people and afterwards, come backstage to the dressing room and talk about who played an A minor when they should have played an A major, and I quickly felt that this was not really the point of touring. So, I got Bobble to print up The Golden Ticket.

'After-Show Pass' it read. 'No autographs. No photographs. Just fun.'

From then on, before the concert, my bandmates would go out into the venue as the audience were arriving, asking fun-looking people if they'd like to come to the afterparty. As a recently retired reconnaissance officer, I briefed the band clearly – don't just dive in on the first pretty girl you see. Stand back in a position of overwatch and observe – her boyfriend might be in the loo. If there's a hot group of girls, ask the least hot one, so you don't look as shallow as you really are. And finally, find the smoking areas, because smokers are risk-takers – and we needed risk-takers.

And for a while there, the whole point of the concert wasn't the music, or the money – it was the afterparty. And we had one every night. In every city. Without fail.

The way we saw it, as guys who were living full-time on the road, the people who were coming backstage were doing us a favour. So, if someone at the afterparty said that their boyfriend was outside, I'd go out and grab him and bring him in. Or if someone said their mother had arrived to take them home, I'd go and grab her and bring her in too. Because who doesn't love a mother-daughter combo?

Then at around 2 a.m. each night, the tour bus would set off for the next city and in the excitement, some people would decide they wanted to come too, and the party would carry on on the bus. But if we've picked you up in Stockholm and you've woken up in Munich, that's quite a journey home. So for those who'd come with us, Bobble would organise plane or train tickets home the next day, arrange taxis and hand them a tour T-shirt each as they left.

My father was the tour bookkeeper, and was always slightly confused by the overall bill for planes, trains and cabs when we lived full-time on a bus. But the end result was that three of my band met the girls of their dreams and lived happily ever after.

The Wives

We were playing in Copenhagen, Denmark, and halfway through the show, I saw a beautiful girl in the audience with a flower in her hair. At the end of the song, as he handed me a new guitar, I pointed her out to my guitar technician, Brian. During the next song, he worked his way through the crowd till he got to her and her friend, handed them two Golden Tickets, and said in his broad Glaswegian accent, 'Do you fancy a backstage?'

Remarkably the girl, a Danish model called Pernille, did. That said, when she got backstage, she looked extremely grumpy. John, my bass player, asked her what was wrong, and she explained that she had gone out that evening thinking she was being taken to a James Bond premiere. She was, therefore, hugely disappointed to see the name 'James Blunt' over the door when she arrived. For this reason alone, John fell in love, and they are now married with two children.

II

On a flight from Sydney to Perth, Australia, the stewardess came over and handed John, the bass player, a piece of paper with her phone number on it. John shrugged – he's married to the Danish model – so Beardy, the keyboard player said, 'I'll have it!'

He left the stewardess a message inviting her to the concert, and she told him backstage that she wanted children immediately, and for that reason alone, Beardy fell in love, and they got engaged a couple of months later, having only met three times. When he called me to say he was engaged, my reaction was genuinely, 'Who to?'

III

On another trip to Perth, a blonde girl called Samantha came backstage after the show and offered Ben, my guitarist, MDMA and for that reason alone, he fell in love, and they got married. After the wedding, Samantha didn't want Ben going on the road any more, so she got him a job down an Australian coal mine. Work conditions were hellish, with temperatures reaching fifty degrees down there. Ben called her after the first day to express how difficult it was.

'Welcome to the real world,' she told him.

Amongst other things, the Romanian thieves stole this irreplaceable tank top.

When your hangover is so bad you need a doctor.

A Tinie Tempah and Snoop Dogg party in the Hard Rock hotel in Ibiza. Soon after the photo was taken, my wife and I were asked to leave the party for wearing too many clothes.

Blunty's Nightclub was voted Ibiza's No.1 club in 2023 and was the only club that stayed open during the pandemic.

This was the last time Nadia was seen alive.

Bobble before his transformation.

Billy meets the
fans in Vegas.

And just like that, the
money started rolling in.

With Paris in Vegas.

Keeping a lookout for icebergs on Diana's boat.

Bono, Larry Mullen and Kid Rock on Diana's boat.

Norberto the policeman returning my father's watch.

Ed Sheeran and his manager, Stuart Camp, when I told them I was writing a book and that they were in it.

This was my hotel in Poland. It is not, as the *Daily Mail* claimed, Auschwitz.

The view from the Pyramid Stage at Glastonbury.

John Garrison's view each night.

The Clintons and The Blounts.

When Ellen DeGeneres asked Justin Bieber what his favourite album was.

'Forgotten how to shave, have we?'

Tara Reid and Jedward.

Me and Mrs. B.

My parents have never been afraid of a bit of cultural appropriation.

Sofia and I got engaged on 21st December 2013 and rather than a ring, I produced this.

The Pussycat Dolls

Around this time, I started dating The Pussycat Dolls.

I met the band on the promo circuit in Europe. They were promoting their song, 'Don't Cha Wish Your Girlfriend Was Hot Like Me' and I was rocking 'You're Beautiful'. Nicole was uber-confident and sexy and had way too many security guards hanging specifically round her, and not the other girls in the band. Weirder still, she always seemed to be trying to escape from them. She would arrange to meet me at her hotel in whichever city we were in, but insist I came in through the back door or fire escape to avoid being seen by the security detail. We'd find ourselves climbing out of windows and on to Italian rooftops overlooking beautiful cities, so that we could make out. On paper that sounds exciting, but snogging someone on the edge of a railing-less lead roof, while keeping your eyes open so you don't fall off and die was not something I could really get into.

The papers reported that I was dating Jessica, the redhead in the band – a story which I now think was leaked on purpose to throw the scent off me and Nicole. And whilst I might have been friends with another member of the band, it wasn't her and it wasn't then. Years later, Ashley and I became friendly, perhaps bonding on the fact that we'd both been ditched by Nicole. Either way, I dated 40 or 60 per cent of the band, depending on who you believe.

I was in Atlanta playing a radio-sponsored concert, with Meat Loaf as my support act, and Nicole flew in to see me. I picked her up and we drove to the radio station where I was giving a live interview before the show. As we walked into the studio, the rock star Gene Simmons of Kiss was there, mid-interview. He looked at me and looked at Nicole, and said on air, 'Hey James, maybe if you played some more balls-out songs, you'd get some more dudes at your show.'

A little confused, I replied, 'Gene, perhaps if you wore a little less make-up, you'd have some more girls at yours.' And with that, we shook hands and he left.

I never got to ask him why I should want more dudes at my show, but it has been a recurring theme. For some reason, men have often mocked me for having more girls in my audience than boys, and it does make me wonder if I got into this whole thing for the wrong reason.

A few months later, as things were really starting to kick off in the US, I played at the House of Blues on the Sunset Strip in Los Angeles. Here's some of the people who came to watch:

Alanis Morissette
Ashton Kutcher
Avril Lavigne
Bono
Brittany Murphy
Carrie Fisher
Daniel Powter
David Duchovny
Demi Moore
Diane Warren
Diane Kruger
Elisha Cuthbert
Jack Black
Jason Mraz
Joaquin Phoenix
Joss Stone
Kate Bosworth
Kelly Osbourne
Kevin Spacey
Larry David
Laura Pausini
Len Blavatnik

Linda Perry
Lindsay Lohan
Maroon 5
Matt Dillon
Matthew McConaughey
Matthew Perry
Max Martin
Mischa Barton
Molly Sims
Nicole Scherzinger
Paul Allen
Penelope Cruz
Petra Němcová
Rob Cavallo
Robbie Williams
Salma Hayek
Scarlett Johansson
Shakira
Tom Whalley
Van Hunt
Vanessa Carlton

After the concert, I was upstairs chatting to Shakira on one side and Robbie Williams on the other, when a huge, heavy-framed African American man approached us, gesturing that he had something to say to me. He bent down to my ear and said in a deep voice, 'Jimmy says, if you fuck Nicole again, he'll kill you.'

Not knowing who he was referring to, I looked up at him, mildly confused and asked, 'Why doesn't Jimmy just tell Nicole not to fuck me again, and then he won't have to kill anyone?'

The man didn't answer. His message passed, he turned away and left.

A bit of light googling the next day turned up that The Pussycat Dolls were signed by music mogul Jimmy Iovine to Interscope Records, and although he was married, there were rumours that he and Nicole were a thing – which would explain the overprotective security assigned to her and not the rest of the band. Nicole and I carried on seeing each other, and I am currently still alive. She was worth dying for.

Many years later, in 2017, I was staying at my friend Diana Jenkins' house in Malibu. Diana is a refugee from Bosnia whose brother was murdered by the Serbs in the war. She'd fled to the UK with five pounds to her name, and married Roger Jenkins – one of the three Barclays bankers who was recently charged and acquitted by the Serious Fraud Office for what they'd have you believe was causing the 2008 financial crash. The weird thing about that was Barclays Bank was the only bank not to need a government bailout, as Diana had negotiated a deal with the Qataris, but her husband was subsequently charged anyway. Roger was credited with inventing something in banking called double-dipping and had become a billionaire as a result. Anyway, Diana divorced him and now she's the billionaire. He went on to date Elle Macpherson, so I don't think his life has been too bad since. I actually went on two dates with Elle as well, but they didn't go well. The paparazzi couldn't get both of us in the same photo – in the pictures, they'd either get me and her knees, or her and my forehead – and she could never hear what I was saying in nightclubs.

Anyway, it was Diana's birthday, and she put on a party, and again, you kind of knew all of the guests, from Kanye and Kim, Orlando and Katie, Ed Sheeran, Courteney Cox, the boys from Snow Patrol, and so on. Diana had spent a ton of money on production, with a crashed aeroplane in the garden and *Avatar* dancers round the pool.

'A-list only, darling!' Diana had said, and invited only fifty famous people in a space that really needed a hundred and fifty to fill it or justify the cost.

As a present for the birthday girl, I'd hired a mini mariachi band consisting solely of dwarves to only play Ed Sheeran songs – although having heard them set up and rehearse, I was anxious as to their reception. As I was staying at the house, I was doing my best to help out by welcoming guests and offering drinks. So, when a bald, older man arrived with a pretty, much younger wife, I greeted them both and offered to get them a drink.

'What's your name?' I asked the man politely.

'Jimmy,' he replied, disinterestedly.

And then it dawned on me.

'Jimmy Iovine!' I exclaimed. 'It's me! James Blunt! Still alive and kicking!'

His faced paled visibly and before his drink arrived, he dragged his new wife away.

At that moment, the mini mariachi band struck up, playing 'Shape of You'. It sounded dreadful. On reflection, it didn't look especially P.C. either. Ed, physically overcome by the sound of his song being defiled, panicked, signalled his security and sprinted out. His entourage of around twenty people, including Courteney Cox and the Snow Patrol gang, scurried out behind him, looking concerned. Seeing the movement, the remaining guests assumed Ed was upset, and as is the Hollywood way, were deeply offended on his behalf. En masse, they put down their drinks and walked out too, leaving me, Diana and the mini mariachi band alone in the garden. Party over, Diana looked at me.

'What the fuck did you just do?' she asked.

Diana's Boat

When she still had money, and I still had fame, Diana Jenkins would take me to the Cannes Film Festival on a superyacht that she'd chartered. It was huge. When someone onshore asked which boat you were on, you could simply reply, 'The big one,' and the team she would assemble would be a gaggle of gay men, a brace of billionaires' wives, some supermodels, Kid Rock and me.

Guests would fight to get on the boat with us. Bono would make an appearance and sing 'Miss Sarajevo' to Diana. The designer Dan Macmillan ended up being hosed down unconscious in the Jet Ski bay, having been sick on someone's bed. If we visited a nightclub, Diana would kidnap all the professional dancers in the club and bring them back to the boat, leaving the nightclub with only the DJ and the punters.

And the boat was a place of fantastic excess. One night, I was given an Adderall, which is medical amphetamine, and later found myself in a pitch-black cabin, lit only by the screen of a BlackBerry mobile phone, held by a voyeuristic billionaire's wife who I'd been overfriendly with the night before. Underneath me was a Russian girl who I knew only as 'Hot For Words'. It took me a moment to realise that the hands pulling my trousers down weren't hers. This was confirmed when I felt a tongue being inserted into my bottom. I looked over my shoulder and, in the half-light, saw it was a married man whose wedding I'd recently played at.

'Help me,' I remember saying to the BlackBerry holder.

Another year, my girlfriend at the time flew in to join us from Switzerland. She'd brought a bag of cash – around forty thousand euros – and I'd told her to drop it on the boat and come and join me at a party where I was with Jean-Claude Van Damme.

At the same time, Diana was flying out by private jet that night to go home to LA, and to get her and her sixteen bags off the boat in time for the flight was a logistical nightmare for the crew.

My girlfriend and I got back to the boat later, and looking in the cabin, found that her bag wasn't there. We asked the crew, and it quickly became apparent that, due to a mix up, it was now onboard a private jet to Los Angeles. And here's the problem. How do you explain that you have a bag of money? And how do you get it back? The flight alone cost a hundred grand and the boat maybe double that, so to ask for it back seemed churlish.

The next day, a Sunday, we were meeting Prince Albert of Monaco, but as her suitcase was now in LA, my girlfriend had nothing to wear. The shops were closed, and she was obviously stressed about what to do, but in a bizarre stroke of luck, I happened to have a spare little black dress in my suitcase. It was genuinely mine – and she was grateful – but it was hard explaining why I had it.

Life with Diana has always been eventful. Once, she picked me up in her private jet from Farnborough to take me to my concert in Sarajevo. On the way, and without warning, we diverted to Milan to pick up the designer Roberto Cavalli. At the airport in Sarajevo, where Diana is considered a hero as she sends a lot of money back, the press had gathered for a press conference. They asked me about my time in the army and experiences in Kosovo, and then they turned to Roberto and asked him why he was here.

'I love the sexy Russian women,' he drawled.

I nudged him and whispered, 'Roberto, we're in Bosnia.'

The Darkness

At the height of *Back to Bedlam*, I toured with a band called The Darkness round Australia and Japan. We weren't playing the same venues and our music is very different – they play comedy rock, while I play comedy soft rock – but we were on the same routing with the same promoters, so each night we'd meet up after our shows for an afterparty, laid on by the record label. They were promoting their second album, which in industry-speak, was bombing. I now know the feeling, but where mine has been a slow and innocuous demise, they were in freefall.

Justin, the singer, had been sleeping with the band's manager, but split with her when their US tour was cancelled. There were rumours of an affair with his brother's girlfriend. And where once he'd started the show by being lowered down on a stuffed tiger whilst playing a guitar solo, with a tighter budget, Justin was now being carried on stage on the production manager's shoulders. Sure, the spandex was still there, but with potbellies and an air of catastrophe. Backstage after the show, someone would have prepared lines of cocaine the full length of the table.

'Cocaine buffet?' they would say. 'Just help yourself.'

The drummer, Ed, who had the shakes before the shows and would have to drink his hands steady, came up to me at a party and opened his jacket to show me some mini bottles of gin and vodka. 'Hey man,' he said. 'If you need a drink, I've got the contents of my minibar.'

'Cheers, Ed,' I said, 'although there's enough booze here to drown in.'

'Well, you know,' he replied. 'Just in case.'

Shelving

After the concert in Sydney, my band and I had a joint afterparty with the Foo Fighters on the top floor of the Intercontinental Hotel. They'd just played the stadium, and I'd played at the arena. We shared a promoter – the late, loud Michael Gudinski – and he'd arranged the joint event.

At some point in the evening, a nineteen-year-old, smoking hot blonde Aussie girl came over to me. The girl whispered in my ear.

'Do you shelve?' she said.

Something about her made me think this was not going to be about DIY.

'Probably,' I replied.

She took my hand and led me to the loos. Locked in the small cubicle together, her blue eyes looking deep into mine, she held up a round, pink pill, which I assumed was ecstasy. She then pulled down her knickers, turned away from me, and looking over her shoulder, told me to stick it up her bottom. I put my middle finger in my mouth for lubrication and, with the same finger, inserted the pill.

At exactly that moment, Dave Grohl of the Foo Fighters entered the next-door cubicle with one of his children, who was feeling ill. I thought I could hear the child sitting on the loo. All Dave heard from my cubicle was a girl's voice saying in a sexy Aussie drawl, 'Your turn.'

She went on to sell the story.

Damon Albarn

Around the same time, the press were starting to give me a hard time back at home, and perhaps worse still, other musicians were starting to join in.

I was on *Later . . . with Jools Holland* – a late addition as Pete Doherty had been kicked off for doing drugs, which was ironic as when I got the call to dash down to the studio, I wasn't exactly sober myself. But the performance and recording went really well, and everyone was thrilled. At the end of each show, they take a photograph of all the musicians together, which is then framed and put on the studio wall. Damon Albarn was on the same episode, but during recording, his management informed the producers that he wouldn't be in the same picture as me. Without explaining to me what was going on, the producers kept me in my dressing room at the end of the show, while they gathered Damon and all the performers together and took the photo. Damon was then led out of the building, and I was brought out for a second photo without him in it. You can guess which picture is on the wall.

At the Q Awards that year, where we were both nominated for the same award, I was seated beside Damon. As he sat down, he turned his seat away and refused to speak to me for the entire three-hour ceremony. When the awards ended, I tapped him on the shoulder and told him that I thought he was a genius, that I loved his album *Demon Days*, and that I was sorry he didn't feel confident enough to talk to me. And with that, carrying the award, I left.

The Brits 2006

I was nominated for five Brits in 2006, which was exciting, but it turned out to be a bittersweet affair.

In the run-up to the awards, Paul Weller issued a statement saying he'd rather eat his own shit than work with me. This caught me by surprise. I'd never asked to work with him – so it seemed more an excuse for him to eat his own shit rather than anything to do with me.

On the red carpet at the awards, perhaps because I was heavily nominated, musicians and bands were asked what they thought of me.

'He's awful posh. I don't like him,' said Charlotte Church.

Lily Allen was more succinct. 'It rhymes with his surname,' she said. Thinking about it now, it was perhaps short-sighted of me when I changed my name from Blount to Blunt.

And so it went on.

I passed Mick Jagger, who was momentarily standing on his

own, and knowing his daughter, Jade, I stuck out my hand and said hello. He looked down at my hand, turned and walked away. Such a public brush-off, captured on camera, obviously stung, although it's worth saying that I probably need to be more understanding – at ninety years old, The Rolling Stones are still out there looking for their big hit, and so it must have been frustrating for him to meet someone who'd had a global megahit right from the start.

At the awards, my father wandered over to Chris Martin, who went to Sherborne School, and told him that the least he could do was to stick up for another posh twat. Chris took to the podium, and said, 'Will everyone stop being so mean to James Blunt?' which although sort of nice of him, didn't particularly help.

I won two awards, one voted for by the public, the other for number of sales. My other nominations were in categories voted for by the industry, so I was in the same boat as Craig David on those ones. Interestingly though, watching my acceptance speeches back, I honestly wanted to punch myself in the face just as much as anyone else, so maybe they were on to something.

Keane were getting stuck in too. We had both been booked to play at the Wireless Festival, but they were the headliners, and through their management, they stuck the knife in and refused to allow me to play. For a moment, they got their way, and the promoters emailed to say I'd been given the boot. But my song just kept getting bigger, and in the end, size does matter. The promoters told Keane to get over it, and I was put back on the bill.

In an interview with *The Sun* ahead of the gig, the journalist asked which band I was least looking forward to bumping into.

'I'm keen not to say,' I replied – which obviously made the headline.

On the day, when I knocked on their dressing room door, stuck my head in and said, 'Good luck today guys, and no hard feelings!' the three band members just stared coldly back. After a moment's thought – they were all public school boys like me – I added, 'We could have a posh-off to settle it if you'd like?'

Kanye West

In America, things were a little different. The song had reached number one there too, and was the first number one by a UK artist since Elton's 'Candle in the Wind'. Oprah had me on her show, and Ellen DeGeneres too – a bunch of times. The same day that Tom Cruise sent me flowers to wish me luck at the Grammys, and the record label handed me a cheque for ten million pounds – that my dad subsequently lost – I got a phone call from Kanye West saying we should work together. I took down his number, thanked him for calling and said I'd be in touch. I never called back. I have terrible imposter syndrome, and just couldn't take the offer seriously. It felt more like a prank call from someone in the industry pretending I was in the industry too. Anyway, he went on to become a white supremacist, so it's probably a good thing.

The Daily Mail

On tour in Europe, as we pulled up to our hotel in Krakow, Poland, the band let out a huge groan. 'Bobble!' we all exclaimed. The hotel was covered in scaffolding and was literally only half built. As we climbed out of the bus, I posed for a picture with the unfinished hotel behind me, and then posted it on Facebook saying, 'errr, my hotel in Poland.'

The next day, the *Daily Mail* published a story saying, 'James Blunt posts picture of himself outside Auschwitz Death Camp pretending it's his hotel in Poland.'

The Poles were able to work out that this was not true – Auschwitz isn't made of modern breezeblocks and scaffolding. The Americans on the other hand awarded me an MTV Award for that year's biggest online fuck-up and removed my songs from US radio for 'offending the Jews'. Even to this day, I'm still asked in interviews in America if I regret offending the Jews, and I feel my mind going in a downward spiral as I ask them,

'Do you even know what Auschwitz looks like!?' I do. I've been there, and it's the closest thing to hell on earth, and it certainly doesn't look like a half-built Holiday Inn.

I got a lawyer to write to the *Mail*, who replied saying that my hotel was *technically* outside Auschwitz. And this is true – it's about a hundred kilometres outside, in the same way that London is about a thousand miles outside.

My wife once spent a weekend with the Rothermeres, who own the *Daily Mail*. Lady Rothermere swore that no one took the paper seriously – so much like this book, buy it and read it if you're fool enough, but don't be fool enough to buy what you read in it.

Interestingly, I once sued the *Daily Mail* for a story they wrote, where they claimed I'd borrowed thirty pounds from a neighbour and not paid the neighbour back. This wasn't true, and it turned out the neighbour didn't live anywhere near me, had never met me, and had never lent me or anyone associated with me any money. But rather than let this very petty story go, I set out the prove it wasn't true, which is quite an undertaking unless you are especially anal. After both parties had run up legal bills of over ten thousand pounds, the paper realised I was a lunatic with nothing better to do, paid my legal costs and issued an apology. And so a fake story about me owing thirty quid ended up costing them over twenty grand.

But there have been darker moments too. My parents were driving in the countryside near their home in Hampshire, when they came across a convertible BMW and a Mini stopped in the road with their doors open. In the passenger seat of the Mini was a young mother screaming. In the back was her six-year-old daughter crying. On the ground between the two cars was a bloodied and unconscious man, and standing over him were two shaven-headed men who were kicking him repeatedly in the head. My father jumped out of the car and confronted the thugs, at one point trying to grab their car keys. For a moment, it looked like they would attack him too, but seeing my mother with her camera out, they jumped in the Beemer and drove off. The police and an ambulance arrived, and it became clear that, had the attackers carried on, the driver of the Mini could well have died. Using the pictures taken by my mother, the police quickly identified and caught the assailants, charged them, and released them pending trial. My parents also agreed to testify as witnesses, but as the men were no longer in custody, asked that their identities be kept confidential until the trial, for fear of reprisals. The police assured them that their details would be protected.

It came as a shock then, when the next day a journalist claiming to write freelance for the *Mail* rang my parents' doorbell. My father was out walking the dog, so my mother answered the door. The journalist said he'd been given her details by the police and was keen to interview her. Sweaty and excited, he explained it would be a fantastic headline reading, 'James Blunt's parents save man from death in violent assault.' In a panic, my mother called me.

From my tour bus in Germany, I called the journalist and pleaded with him not to endanger my parents. I couldn't have been more humble and conciliatory. After all, we were at his mercy.

'I'm on my knees,' I told him. 'I'm really begging you to not put my parents in danger.'

'Don't you call me and try to intimidate me,' the journalist sneered. 'It's a great fucking story.'

After a bunch of expensive legal letters, the paper didn't print the story – and there's the lesson. The law doesn't protect you from the papers. Only money does.

The News of the World Girls

The *News of the World* hacked my phone. At the time, I didn't know I was being hacked. It was at the height of my fame and my phone kept ringing from a withheld number. I'd pick up and whoever was calling would just hang up. I thought maybe I'd given my phone number to a girl in a club, and she'd told her mates, and they thought it would be funny to drunkenly call to see if it was really me. Either way, it happened a lot and I just felt like I was being harassed or bullied. I was also really embarrassed to admit this was going on to either of my friends.

At the time, I was seeing Nicole Scherzinger, and she would occasionally call on a withheld number and I'd be so paranoid that I'd hand the phone to my mate Billy and ask him to tell whoever was calling to fuck off. She found that quite distressing.

Years later, the police got in touch and explained what had been going on. They sent a copy of the private detective Glenn Mulcaire's notebook, which had my details in it. On a page with my name at the top, he had my phone number, Orange account number, PIN number and what I think was a contact name at Orange.

The police also sent redacted copies of the *News of the World*'s internal emails relevant to my case, but as I was away on tour, these were sent to my parents' house. The most embarrassing story was about a girl called Emma Kearney and a mate of hers, who it transpired were on the *News of the World*'s payroll to go out and fuck celebrities. The girls would bring the men back to Emma's studio flat in Notting Hill, which had a fold-down bed, film the encounter, and then hand it over to the paper. The girls were hot, and I'd met them, and sure enough, I'd done the deed, and now, in these emails that my mother was reading, the *News of the World*'s editor Andy Coulson – who at one point worked as a No. 10 advisor to David Cameron – was discussing how best to portray my orgasm.

'He'd sing her name twice,' he wrote.

'Emma! Emma!' it read in the paper.

I googled Emma Kearney and found similar kiss-and-tell stories by her and her mate with Shane Warne, Enrique Iglesias, John Terry and me – and out of all of them, I was last.

A Classist Gimp

Over the next few years, I was the go-to target for the press. I'd always been advised to bend over and take it – which as a public school boy, I'm pretty good at. But when Labour politician Chris Bryant joined in too, I could bend over no more.

I'd never heard of Bryant before, but he gave an interview to *The Guardian*, saying that 'we mustn't have a culture dominated by James Blunt and his ilk'. By my ilk, he means posh people. Before my mother could email him, I wrote a childish reply, and they kindly published it in *The Guardian* too. For better or worse, it read as follows:

Dear Chris Bryant MP,
You classist gimp.
    I happened to go to a boarding school. No one there helped me get into the music business. I bought my first guitar with money I saved from holiday jobs (sandwich packing!). I was taught the only four chords I know by a friend.

When I left the army, everyone I met in the British music industry told me there was no way I would succeed because I was too posh. One record company even asked if I could speak in a different accent. (I told them I could do Pakistani.) Now I've managed to break through, I'm still scoffed at for being too posh.

And then you come along, looking for votes, telling working class people that posh people like me don't deserve it. But it's your populist, envy-based ideas which make our country crap, far more than me and my shit songs, and plummy accent.

I got signed in America, where they don't even understand what you mean by me and 'my ilk', you prejudiced wazzock, and I worked my arse off. What you teach is the politics of jealousy. Rather than celebrating success, you talk about how we can hobble that success and 'level the playing field'. What you've failed to realise is that the head start my school gave me in the music business, where the vast majority of people are not from public school, is to tell me that I should aim high. Perhaps that protected me from your narrow-minded, self-defeating, remove-the-'Great' from 'Great Britain' thinking, which is simply to look at others' success and say, 'it's not fair.'

Up yours,

James Cucking Funt

If I'd been cooler, I would have just tweeted: 'Chris, you don't help people get to the top of the tree by giving them a bow and arrow. Give them a ladder instead.'

As it was, the letter caused a bit of a reaction.

The cover of that month's *New Statesman* was an illustration of me surrounded by David Cameron, Boris Johnson, Benedict Cumberbatch, Eddie Redmayne, Chris Martin and Damian Lewis, all wearing tails coats and drinking champagne. I was six inches shorter and in the middle of this ghastly public-school circle jerk, like a new boy sucking up to the seniors.

I posted the picture online, saying, 'I won't be picking up the soap when this party moves to the showers.'

One person was offended – a straight woman called Lisa. She took to Twitter to voice her outrage, posting three angry tweets. But that's all it takes nowadays. The *Daily Mail* labelled it a 'Twitter Storm' and contacted Peter Tatchell, the gay rights activist, and Stonewall for comment, who didn't seem as offended as they'd hoped, but it was enough for the paper to run a headline claiming I'd offended gay people – meaning straight Lisa.

But here's the thing – after sixteen years in all-male institutions, the simple fact is that I probably have more experience in all-boys showers than Lisa, and maybe even Peter Tatchell, although perhaps not as much as the whole of Stonewall. But from that, I can say that gay people don't have a monopoly on gay experiences. Posh people have always had a slice of that pie too. I mean, what do you think the P stands for in LGBTPQIA+?

Years later, I would find myself in another Twitter storm when I was trying to promote my sixth album. I did an interview for *The Independent* newspaper. It was at the time that the Tories under Theresa May, and Parliament as a whole, were in a painful limbo about what to do after the Brexit referendum. *The Independent* newspaper has a Brexit-triggered readership, and so the journalist, called Ed Cumming, kept asking me about Brexit. Now, I'm trying to flog an album to anyone with bad enough taste to buy it – whatever their Brexit persuasion. But Cumming persisted, and when it came to a question about the impact of Brexit on my touring, I gave what I thought was a moderate answer:

'It's up to politicians to decide what they want to do now and move us forward so that we can start making plans – I'm heading out on tour next year, and we need to know what the impact of any post-Brexit deal might be on that. Whatever cock-up they concoct, it's not going to stop us going out on the road – although it's likely to be more paperwork for my tour manager – but either way, it would be good to know.'

And *The Independent* ran the headline:

'Blunt says get the fuck on with Brexit because our lives aren't going to change!'

And so, with this headline, a Twitter storm of angry *Independent* readers, all with the surname, Fbpe (Follow Back Pro EU), wet themselves. After three days of trending on Twitter, I thought I'd respond and so, much to my manager's horror – I posted this on Twitter:

Hey @edcumming and @Independent – you cunts!
In an interview about my new album (out on Friday!), you kept asking about Brexit. I gave you a reasonable answer – that politicians, whatever they choose, should make a decision and move us forward now, as this state of limbo is killing us. I live in Spain, so it would be nice to know. As to how it will end, I don't know, but I guessed the EU/UK will probably fudge something together, and we'll have to muddy through, like we always do. A pretty pragmatic answer from someone who's touring Europe in February (tickets on sale now!). So how does the article end up saying 'James Blunt says get the fuck on with Brexit because our lives aren't going to change'?

Within minutes, the editor of *The Independent* called my publicist, and said that if I didn't remove the tweets, *The Independent* newspaper would declare war on me. He also said that Cumming had received death threats, which made me happy that at least he and I were now in the same boat – although I'd received several thousand more than the four nasty comments he'd received about his weight.

My publicist called my manager, and my manager called me, but I declined to remove the tweets. My publicist actually said she would resign if I didn't remove them, which slightly showed which side her bread was buttered, but I was enjoying myself, and sent her and him a message saying, 'Hey guys. Chill. You bitch-slapped me. I bitch-slapped you back. Get over it.'

And they did.

That December, I was invited to Piers Morgan's Christmas Drinks Party at The Scarsdale Tavern. I arrived a little drunk, and the first person I bumped into was the editor of the MailOnline. I asked him if he wanted a blowjob, as I'd just had my teeth sharpened. Next up, I bumped into Ed Cumming, who snivelled on about how he doesn't write the headline, and how he hoped that the publicity had helped me sell lots of albums. It obviously didn't, you gammy turd. And then I bumped into Emily Maitlis. She asked me if I'd seen the interview she did with Prince Andrew and I told her I'd actually been at Prince Andrew's house when the interview was aired, which is true. And then I left.

Blunty's Nightclub

Yeah, so having become a national pariah, I upped sticks and moved to Ibiza. I bought a house on a hill so that I can see the enemy coming, and wrote songs with titles like 'How Did I Become Barry Manilow?'.

When he heard I'd moved to Ibiza, Noel Gallagher sold his house and left the island, saying he couldn't live there any more in the knowledge that I was down the road writing my shitty songs. House prices rocketed and everyone who was anyone flooded to the island, but I honestly couldn't say if that was because I'd arrived, or because Noel had left. But I get his point, and although my music is as limp as lettuce, I actually love dance music and nightclubs. The lead single on my second album, '1973', is about Pacha, the island's most famous club, which opened that same year. Although the song only reached number four in the UK, it was a global number one and Pete Tong remixed it and played it in Pacha during his residency there. And no matter what was going on in the media back at home, dancing in an Ibizan super club to my own song was pretty cool.

At the time, I was going out with Petra Němcová, a supermodel whose fiancé was killed in the tsunami of 2004. Her story is harrowing. They were in a cabana near the beach in Khao Lak, Thailand, when the wave hit and were both swept out of the window. Petra was found eight hours later, naked, her pelvis broken, clinging to a tree. Her fiancé's body was found three months later. Petra is a good human being. She works for charity, doesn't drink or do drugs, her catchphrase was 'love, light and happiness', and when she meets anyone, she kisses them three times, as the Dutch do – although she's Czech.

It's fairly evident, then, that God does not exist, because the next person Petra ended up dating was me.

As a housewarming present, Petra bought a running machine. We kept it down by the pool house, and she'd be on it every night, while I sat on the roof of the main house getting drunk and high with my friends, occasionally waving down to her sweating away. When we split up, my friends and I got the running machine out and racked up a line of blow along the entire length of the treadmill. I then knelt down at the end of the machine, nose ready, while someone else set the speed to fifteen kilometres an hour and hit 'GO'.

It was a time of great experimentation. My doctor at the time decided he wanted to try having cocaine blown up his arse through a straw. He thought I should administer, as I have a good set of lungs. I also own a Household Cavalry trumpeter's mouthpiece, which seemed like the perfect implement for insertion and delivery. So I packed the trumpet mouthpiece with blow, while he lubed up his ring with butter. He then bent over with his hands on his knees, and having inserted the mouthpiece inside his arse, I knelt down behind him, lips pursed, and at that moment, his girlfriend walked in.

There aren't many ways to explain what you're doing in these circumstances.

'Err, it is how it looks,' I told her.

This wasn't actually my first rodeo. I'd had a similar experience some months earlier when a rather beautiful forty-year-old woman with an amazing figure asked if I would do the same to her. We were at a party, and had neither mouthpiece nor butter, so I got a straw from the bar. In the bathroom, I thought I'd pushed the straw in deep enough, but it turned out I was wrong. As I blew, instead of going up her bottom, the contents of the straw bypassed her ring, followed the curvature of her buttocks, and came straight back all over my face, like I'd faceplanted in flour.

This was about the same time that my friends and I discovered you can pour vodka on the hot stones in my sauna and the resulting alcoholic vapour gets you all completely hammered. A note of safety, however – I did it once where the vodka reached the electric heating coil under the stones, setting the spirit alight. The flames swept up the wooden walls and across the wooden ceiling, which caused quite a stampede.

I also had a giant fig tree in the middle of my garden, which must have been over a hundred years old. People would come back to my house for afterparties when the clubs closed, and would end up like zombies circling round under the fig tree, reaching up and eating the figs. Watching this from a daybed as the sun came up one morning, and while everyone else was talking about mushroom chocolate and hash brownies, I had a brainwave – *acid figs*. I consulted a well-informed man from Amsterdam, who furnished me with several litres of liquid acid, costing several thousands of pounds. Over a period of three years, instead of water, I fed the fig tree liquid acid and waited for it to come up. On the fourth year, the tree stopped producing figs. I wondered if it was going through an existential crisis or thought it was a fern. By the seventh year, it was dead.

I built a nightclub at the end of my garden. Admittedly, it's perhaps more like a teenager's disco than a club, with a smoke machine, lasers, a disco ball and some second-hand flashing lights that I'd bought from Ritzy's nightclub in Swindon. But I tell people it's a club, and there's a big neon sign in it that my band gave me saying, 'Blunty's Nightclub – Where Everybody's Beautiful' – and if you drink enough, they are.

That first year, a vodka company called Oval sent me five hundred bottles of vodka for free, and then Puff Daddy-Puffy-P. Diddy-Diddy sent me four hundred bottles of Cîroc. Of the nine hundred bottles of vodka, we drank fifty the first year, which meant we had another seventeen years' worth to go. As I write to you now, it's 2023, and I'm holding the last half-full bottle in my hand.

There's also a mannequin on the door called Svetlana. She stands behind a red rope, holding a clipboard with my friends' names on it. My wife hates her because I sometimes come back with a new dress, and my wife gets excited, and I have to tell her that it's actually for Svetlana. But Svetlana is not the first mannequin to work the door of my club. Before her, I used to employ Nadia, but one night, when Nadia was the last girl standing, my mate Billy broke her back somehow. Anyway, I buried Nadia in a shallow grave in the forest behind the house, wearing a wedding dress that an ex-girlfriend had left when we split up. I left the tips of Nadia's righthand fingers sticking out of the ground slightly, so that in fifty years or so, someone might stumble upon them, and they'll dig them up and find a mannequin buried in a wedding dress, and wonder what the fuck is going on, and someone will tell them that there was this weird minor pop star who used to live at the house, who apparently died with his trousers round his ankles and a lemon in his mouth some years earlier.

Buying a mannequin is a curious thing. You go to the mannequin shop, and they line them all up with the plainest on the left, increasing in attractiveness till you reach the hottest on the right. Correspondingly, the one on the far left is the cheapest, and the one on the far right is the most expensive – so quite true to life. I asked how much the one on the right was.

'Twenty thousand euros,' the saleswoman said.

Holy fuck, I thought. But being a pop star, it's important not to react.

'Oh right,' I replied cooly. 'And the one beside her?'

'Nineteen thousand, nine hundred euros.'

Now feeling slightly trapped, and not wanting to appear cheap, I chose the one standing just right of the midway mark of the line of mannequins. She was a pretty but slightly detached brunette, who set me back nine thousand euros, and I named her Nadia.

Some years later, after I'd buried Nadia, I returned to the same mannequin shop, and again, they lined them up for me. Not wanting the people working in the shop to think my career was on anything but an upwards trajectory, I bought a mannequin slightly further over to the right than the last time, and that's Svetlana.

Frustratingly, they keep the hottest mannequin in the shop window all year round, and to this day, I still drive past the shop to see her and wish for one more big hit so that I can afford her.

Ibiza suits me, and whilst I hope not for a while, it is where I plan to die. In the fifteenth century, Nostradamus said, 'Ibiza will be the ultimate refuge on earth', and he's not wrong. My neighbour here is Jesus. He's been chilling on the island for over two thousand years and we often have lunch with him on Easter Sunday when the rest of the world is looking for him. He plays trumpet in a band, and in the summer, he and his bandmates, who are all pretty old, play in hotel restaurants for tourists.

'I only fuck Spanish women in the winter,' he told me with a giggle.

The Paparazzi

When I was going out with Petra, I ran over a paparazzi in my car. I don't mean over his toes. I mean completely over him. We were leaving Bryan Lourd's Oscars party in Beverly Hills – Bryan was Carrie Fisher's gay ex-husband with whom she'd had Billie, her daughter. He's also the head of CAA, the acting agency, so his Oscars parties are a hot ticket. Anyway, I was driving, and as we pulled out of the driveway of Bryan's house, the paps surrounded our car. They were banging on my window shouting, 'Hey cunt!' and on her side, one of them was shouting, 'Hey Petra, we're gonna be jerking off over you tonight!' They do this to try to get a reaction from the celebrity – and a more valuable photo if the tactic works. They were on the bonnet and all round the car like a swarm, and through all the banging and shouting, one pap by the front-right headlight, throwing his arms up in the air in an overexaggerated manner and pretending to lose balance, intentionally fell in front of the car. Well, we were on a road,

205

and by my reckoning he should have been on the sidewalk. And having run over people in a tank and they survived unharmed, I made a quick assessment of my Toyota Camry rental car, and still smiling for the cameras, I gently pressed the throttle. At about two miles an hour, we went bu-boom, bu-boom over him, and still at two miles an hour, I drove slowly away.

The police and an ambulance were called, and in between the 911 call and help arriving, the paparazzo was filmed rubbing his leg hard, with whomever was filming saying, 'Rub it harder, man. You've got to make it look redder!' The pap also got up occasionally to take pictures of other celebrities leaving the party. Amazingly, his friend posted a video of this online, and so when the paparazzo sued me for actual bodily harm, I counter-sued for reckless endangerment and won.

Leaving an event the next day, the paps were all shouting at me, 'You nearly killed our friend last night!'

'Come on then!' I shouted back. 'Throw yourselves into the road!' I was heavily influenced by *Withnail* as a teenager.

Even though my home in Ibiza is off the beaten track, the paps soon found out where it was and started coming to the house. I have pretty old-fashioned views about privacy, so when the first one came up my dirt track on a scooter, I jumped out of a tree and grabbed his helmet as he drove past. His head and then his body came with it, while the scooter carried on. I buried him in a shallow grave beside Nadia, but without the fingers sticking out.

A few weeks later, when Petra and I were lying by the pool, my gardener, Ronnie, came screaming into the garden.

'Paparazzi! Paparazzi!' he was shouting.

I looked over to see that two photographers were actually in the garden photographing us. In the ensuing commotion, they ran off and jumped into their car by the gate and I jumped into mine, and we had a car chase down the driveway and on to the main road. I had a really beaten-up old Golf, so didn't mind bumping the back of their car, which I could see made them a little distressed, particularly at higher speeds. When we got to busier roads, however, I broke off the chase. I had taken their number plate and called an English security guard called Joe, who had told me that if I needed anything sorted, I should give him a call. Joe took the details, and within a few hours, called back. The number plate was registered to a rental car company, and after a phone call to them, Joe had an address of a rental apartment in Ibiza Town.

Joe wasn't keen on me relaying the next bit of the story . . . So the story's the same, but I've changed Joe's name to Bob.

At around six the next morning, Bob and a colleague went round to the apartment. They rang the bell and knocked on the door, and when it opened, they went in, in a way he described as hard and fast. Holding the man who'd answered the door up against the wall, and rousing his friend who was still in bed, they demanded the men give back what they'd taken from James Blunt's house.

'What do you mean?' the photographers were screaming, terrified. 'We didn't take anything.'

'He wants his fucking privacy back!' Bob screamed in their faces.

After that, the paparazzi stopped coming.

Fans

I get how you can be fanatical about The Beatles or Justin Bieber, but you have to be pretty deranged to be a fan of mine. Nevertheless, I have a couple, and for that, I am grateful.

Except one of them scares me.

I don't know her name, but she first showed up at a gig in St. Louis, Missouri, in 2007. After the show, I signed autographs and took photos, but then a middle-aged woman followed me and Bobble back to the tour bus. She was asking some personal questions and was slightly on edge, and although Bobble and I were as polite as possible, when we got to the bus, I was out of there.

She was back in 2010, telling the band that she was a friend of mine and needed to speak to me. A wildness in her eyes, and the fact that she wouldn't divulge how we were friends, or have my phone number, made them cynical, and they warned security that we had a live one.

But at the 2013 gig in a casino in Atlantic City, things were more intense. The band had already warned me that she was there.

'It's me again,' she said ominously to them. 'Remember me?'

They did – but not in a good way.

When I came out after the show to sign autographs, she was there, pushing past others and insisting we speak privately. I asked if we could just speak then and there, but she demanded time alone with me. I really didn't want to be alone with her. With the last autograph signed, I gestured to Bobble and security and we walked away. As I was led through the casino to the lifts, she followed close behind, still talking to me, and as we got to the doors, I stopped.

'Please don't follow me any more. It's making me uncomfortable,' I implored.

'How dare you!' she spat, seething. 'You know me. You've been to my house dozens of times!'

Oh, wow. Have I? I thought. *Is this an old family friend who I've failed to recognise?* I was completely stunned.

'It's me!' she went on angrily. 'The subway. New York. Nineteen eighty-four.'

'The girl from "You're Beautiful"?' I asked.

'EXACTLY!' she shouted.

Just in time, the lift doors closed, leaving her outside.

We would meet again in Boston in 2017. She was outside a venue called the House of Blues all day, asking the band to tell me that she was there. She'd handed John, my bass player, a fifty-page folder documenting her and my life together, including details of how I'd stalked her for years, hung round outside her house, and followed her on the subway in 1984. Fortunately, we were in America, where it's nigh on impossible for angry nutters to get hold of guns, so I had nothing to worry about, but as I stared out at the audience that night, unable to spot where she was, I did occasionally wonder if I'd hear or feel the shot first.

Afterwards, I was escorted to the bus, and as I boarded, she came screaming out of the darkness.

'You know my name!' she shouted.

I didn't, and I don't want to.

But just in case you're reading this – in 1984 I would have been ten years old, the first time I visited the States was in 2002, and I only sang the word 'Subway' because 'She smiled at me on the Underground' doesn't really roll off the tongue . . .

Omar the Pharmacist

We never really knew if Omar the Pharmacist was an arms dealer or a mobile phone salesman. All that really mattered was that he had the best table in all the nightclubs in Ibiza, was extremely naughty, and very, very generous. I knew he was Iraqi with British citizenship. In the grittiest club, Amnesia, he had the private table on the balcony overlooking the dancefloor, beside the near-naked dancers. Behind his table, a door led to his own private chillout room with sofas, sound system and bathroom – with a shower. In Pacha, he had his own private loo in which he'd installed aircon. Wherever he went, a trail of young, cool partygoers followed, and maybe as an indication of his lifestyle, he was the only person on the planet my wife specifically said was not allowed to come to my stag do.

In September 2015, years after I'd met him, when I was living in Sydney and working as an *X Factor* judge, Omar's wife Susan called me.

'He's been taken!' she said in her Brummie accent. 'He hasn't rung for three days.'

'Who took him?' I asked. 'And where was he when you last spoke to him?'

'I don't know,' she sobbed. 'He phoned from Istanbul airport, transiting to Beirut.'

We hung up and I immediately called Omar's girlfriend.

'He's been taken!' she cried. 'He hasn't rung for three days. All three of his phones are switched off.'

Weirdly, if someone you know is taken hostage, I'm the person to call. My wife set up a law firm with Cherie Blair, so we called Tony, and he assigned us the country's most senior diplomat to help. My uncle, David, works for a security firm called Control Risks in Iraq, as does my older cousin, who also happens to be called James Blount. Back in the eighties, James Blount Senior was an undercover operator in Afghanistan, and has great pictures of himself in local garb watching the Soviets at Bagram airfield during the war. Nowadays, he specialises in kidnap for ransom, so James assigned us a kidnap-for-ransom negotiator, and David connected us to their Middle East office. Whilst Susan called the police, I phoned the embassy and tweeted the ambassador in Beirut, both of whom got in touch within the hour. And my best friend, Rupert, is in the Special Forces, so I called him to discuss how best to track Omar's three mobile phones.

That afternoon, the Foreign Office called me.

'How do you know this man?' they asked.

'Well,' I said, 'I met him in the loos in Pacha nightclub in Ibiza. His has air conditioning.'

Silence.

'Listen,' I went on, 'I don't think he's a murderer or anything, but he definitely has the propensity to get himself into trouble.'

Apple emailed me a release form so the authorities could remotely access my phone, and to this day, ghost messages come and go, as if someone else got to them first.

And then we waited.

Then, on the seventh day after Omar's disappearance, Susan and his girlfriend received an identical email:

> From: Ahmend Jad
> Subject: Mr Ommar
> 2 October 2015 08:03
> Mr ommar is OK. he will be London in few days.

Now, Susan is from Birmingham, and pulls no punches, so without consulting any of the experts in our newly built hostage negotiation team, she replied herself.

> From: Susan
> To: Ahmend Jad
> Subject: Re: Mr Ommar
> 2 October 2015 08:19
> Who is this? I have a Prime Minister, the Ambassador, the SAS, the Foreign Office, MI6 and the police investigating his disappearance. We're coming for you.

Ahmend replied within two hours.

> From: Ahmend Jad
> To: Susan
> Subject: Re: Re: Mr Ommar
> 2 October 2015 10:14
> Not good make noise. today Friday holiday for government. maybe tomorrow finish.

And then on the eighth day, Susan received this:

> From: Omar
> To: Susan
> Subject: Hello!!
> 3 October 2015 08:36
> Hi Baby!! Ordeal is over, will get my phones and my laptop back tonight, and hopefully be on a flight back to London tomorrow. Sorry to make you worry, can't wait to see you both.

And then on the ninth day, Susan got a phone call. It was Omar.

'Hey Baby! I'm at Gatwick! I'm so sorry for everyth . . . Oh, hang on,' Omar's voice stuttered. 'There's a bit of a welcoming party, habibi. I'll call you back.' And then he hung up.

I didn't see Omar again until 2017, but when I did, he sat me down and thanked me for calling every agency under the sun. I was, as he understood, just trying to save his life. That said, he told me that in doing so, I had fucked him. Hoping to keep under the radar, he'd paid for his own release, and had hoped to slip back home unnoticed. However, thanks to me, every agency I had called had met him at the airport and wanted to know exactly what had gone on and why, and everything about him generally. This apparently cost him considerably more than the ransom. The upshot is that Omar no longer has the best tables in Ibiza. You can find him and me at the bar instead.

Paris

I am a Paris Hilton fan. She is a sweet, generous person, and I've always enjoyed her company. She can be silly – like when she went to a nightclub holding a bible after she'd been convicted of drink driving – but she can be highly perceptive and self-aware too. And while some write her off as an airhead, she's made a multimillion-pound business out of people's obsession with celebrity. If you think about it, that girl walked so the Kardashians could run.

The final concert of my first world tour – which was two-and-a-half-years on the road – was in The Joint in the Hard Rock Hotel in Vegas. My mates, including Billy and Nin, had flown in from all over the world and Paris came too. Early on in my career, I'd told my fans that Billy moderated my website's chatroom – it was in fact me all along – so when they heard he was coming, they were all super excited to finally meet him. My tour manager had organised for some dancing girls, dwarves and chickens to be released on to the stage during the last three songs, so the show ended in mayhem, as I was trying to hit a gong that had been lowered down from the ceiling while trying not to squash the dwarves or hit the girls, who were all moving, unrehearsed, around the stage. After the show, Paris took us out on the town, and let me be clear – there is no better human being in the world to take you out in Vegas than Paris Hilton. We went from club to club, and VIP table to VIP table, with five seven-foot tall bouncers, who would hold your hand as we pushed through the queues, guide you to the loos through the crowds, hold your willy when you needed to pee, and zip up your trousers if you were too drunk to do it yourself.

Our last stop was a new nightclub called Tao. It was the place to be and on everyone's lips. That night, Jay-Z was launching an album there, and we were given the table bang in front of the stage. Its three large faux-leather sofas should only have fitted about twenty of us, but we must have been forty strong, packed in and on each other. Owen Wilson was asking about Sheryl Crow, my mate Billy was getting selfies with Ron Jeremy the porn star, and Paris and I were drinking vodka straight from the bottle. And then Jay-Z came out and it kicked off. For the whole four songs, the club went mad. Jay-Zed was king. It was banging. But as it ended, and Jay-Z walked off the stage, the DJ put on Paris Hilton's new single 'Stars Are Blind'. Hearing her song, Paris stepped up, over the back of the sofa and on to the stage. She took the mic from Jay-Z's hand, and with the mic still on, started singing along over her own track.

Halfway through the song, she threw up.

The club emptied. My mate Nin, who always misses the best bits in life, came out of the loo and phoned me saying, 'Mate, where's everyone gone?'

I didn't see Paris for a while after that, but when I returned to Los Angeles a few months later to record my second album, Paris and I hooked up and sort of had a thing together. One night, we went to Teddy's nightclub in The Roosevelt Hotel, and at closing time, she invited a ton of people back to her house off Sunset Boulevard for an afterparty. I could name just about everyone in there, from Leonardo, to Cameron Diaz, the surfer Kelly Slater and so on, and because of all the famous people in the house, there were a ton of paparazzi hanging round outside. After a couple of hours, no one had left the party, so the paps called the police and made a noise complaint, pretending to be the neighbours. Sure enough, the police turned up to shut us down, and the paps got ready to take their photos. When the doorbell rang, because I was staying at the house, I answered the entry-phone. Seeing it was the police, I went back into the sitting room, where everyone was, and turned off the music.

'Hey guys. The police are at the door,' I said. 'I think the least famous person should go and answer it.'

They all looked back at me, quizzically.

'Okay,' I said, 'I'll go.'

Lindsay

Somewhere along the way, again while I was recording my second album, Lindsay Lohan and I also had a thing. I'm not exactly sure what you'd call it, but it was a thing. My main confusion was she also seemed to be going out with the DJ Samantha Ronson at the time, but I like to watch, so I didn't really mind. Samantha did mind, however, and didn't like me at all.

Lindsay and I met in a club called Les Deux, which the Americans pronounce Lay Do. The club owner, Sylvain, had given me my own permanent table in there, and had furnished it with a plaque saying:

James Blunt
Table 105

I still have the plaque, just to remind me that, once, I was big enough to have my own table in a Los Angeles nightclub.

218

When Lay Do finally closed in 2010, Sylvain opened another club and called it Warwick, which the Americans pronounce Worewick, so I'm guessing he was just trolling his fellow Los Angelians.

But in 2007, Les Deux was raging. Britney Spears, Nicole Richie, Paris Hilton and Ashton Kutcher were permanent fixtures. Sylvain would come out front to bring me and my friends in, so avoiding the queues and paparazzi, and lead us to the table. One night, sitting on the back of the sofa, a crowd round us, a pretty girl beside me took my phone out of my hand, typed in a number, and pressed call. The phone in her other hand rang. She handed mine back to me, and twenty seconds later, my phone buzzed. The message read, 'Let's get out of here.'

I typed in two letters and pressed send.

'OK.'

Out on the street, all hell broke loose. We scrambled into my cheap, white Toyota hire car – the paparazzi in a frenzy. As I drove us out of the parking lot with the paps chasing behind on foot, camera flashes everywhere, the girl climbed out of the passenger seat, straddled me, and shoved her tongue down my throat – and that's how I met Lindsay Lohan.

With a trail of paparazzi still behind, we drove to The Roosevelt Hotel. Ditching the car outside and the paps in the lobby, we took the lift up to Jamie Foxx's room, where he and a few friends were drinking. Lindsay took me into the loo and offered me a line, and afterwards I let her go into the hotel room, as I needed a party poo. I'm pretty fast in these situations, and in the bathroom, all seemed to have gone to plan, until I pressed the flush. Instead of the water and its contents disappearing out of my life, the water started to rise – and fast. Panic rising with it, and no way to stop it, the water rose and rose – till, remarkably, it reached the very rim of the bowl, and thank God, stopped. I stared at my crap spinning gracefully round the edge.

I daren't flush the loo again. It would have flooded the room. Putting my hand into the bowl, through the cold water, and feeling deep into the U-bend, whilst trying to avoid touching my creation, I could find no blockage. I began to imagine the humiliation I was about to endure, and Jamie Foxx and his friends' faces as I asked him to call reception for help.

I needed a rabbit out of a hat.

Back at university, I was in a band called Limp Willy and The Disappointments with the adventurer Bear Grylls, and at times like these, I often ask myself, 'What would Bear do?' But in this exceptional situation, I decided I should actually ask him. I pulled out my phone and began texting.

'Hey Bear. Emergency here. I'm in a hotel bathroom with a blocked loo and an angry floater. No windows. Room full of people outside. Need suggestions.'

'Morning Blunty,' came a timely reply. 'You tried putting your hand down the bog?'

'Tried that. No joy,' I replied.

'Transfer floater to a bin?' he suggested.

'No bag,' I informed him.

'Last resort, mate. Eat it.'

'Eat the shit?' I replied.

'Do it.'

Now slightly regretting texting him in the first place, I reached down, picked the shit up in my hand and ate it. Job done, I brushed my teeth with Jamie Foxx's toothbrush, and emerged from the bathroom, vaguely triumphant.

Thirty minutes later, Lindsay and I jumped in the car and headed back to hers. By now, it was late, but she'd invited a few people over. They were all pretty messy, and I didn't know anyone else there other than Lindsay. I couldn't even tell if they were her friends. Anyway, I was recording the next day, so at around 3 a.m., I told her I was heading home. Lindsay begged me not to leave. She told me that I should just climb into her bed and she promised me that she'd be there in half an hour. Taking me by the hand, she led me to the bedroom, put me in her bed, kissed me, and left, and I fell asleep with the sound of the ongoing party in the background.

I don't know how long it was. It could have been forty minutes – it could have been two hours – but at some point, the door opened and the lights came on. I looked up, expecting to see a hot, drunk girl about to climb into bed with me. Instead, the face of Lindsay's huge African American security guard greeted me.

'Hey James, you've got to go now,' he said.

'What?' I replied, confused.

'Lindsay says you've got to go,' he explained.

'What do you mean? Where is she?' I asked.

'She's gone,' he replied.

Sure enough, the apartment was empty.

I got up, got dressed, and drove home.

Four days later, Lindsay called to say there was a party in the Hollywood Hills. It was a Sunday night, and again I was in the studio the next day, so I told her that it wasn't going to be a big night for me. I went to the party early, and by the time Lindsay arrived, it was almost time for me to think about leaving. She was relaxed – she said I should just get in her car and the driver would take me to hers. She called ahead to get security to let me in and said she would just meet me there later. So I got in her car, and security let me in to her apartment, and I got undressed, climbed into bed and fell asleep.

At some point, hours later, the lights came on.

'Hey, James,' said the deep, warm, familiar voice.

'No way,' I said.

'Yeah man,' said her security guard. 'Lindsay says you've got to go.'

He patted me on the back on my way out.

It was a time when life in West Hollywood was getting pretty messy. Britney was being pursued until she had a public meltdown. Paris had been done for driving under the influence and was doing jailtime. I'd had my huge first album, and where once I needed to climb fire escapes to sneak into nightclubs, I was now being swept in through the front door and past the queues like Hollywood royalty. My friends and I would be out at a club every night, and then on to an afterparty every night too. There literally weren't enough days in the week. It was pre-Uber, and with cabs few and far between, everyone drank and drove in LA – and the paps were a nightmare. But where they were all over me like a bad rash, they were all over Lindsay like piranhas. Leaving clubs was hectic, but the car chases, on the other hand, were dangerous. By morning, pictures and videos from the night before would be sprawled across the internet, usually with unpleasant commentary. Eventually, my manager phoned.

'Just do me a favour, James,' he implored in his Boston accent. 'The next time Lindsay suggests you go to an afterparty in her car, will you just say no, and tell her you'll meet her there instead?'

That night at 1.30 a.m. in Les Deux, when Lindsay told me we were going, and to get in the car, Todd's words in my head, I said I'd catch her up. She got in her little black Merc and took off. The paps took off with her, chasing her through the streets of Hollywood, jumping red lights as they went. On Sunset Boulevard in Beverly Hills, she lost control of the car, first hitting the curb and then a tree. The car ended up on the sidewalk with a badly damaged front end and steam venting from the cracked radiator. The paparazzi swarmed round the crash, like they did with Princess Diana. Lindsay got out and fled.

Posted online that night, what they filmed was a terrible sight – an injured young woman in distress, pursued by a pack of bloodthirsty men. It's a scenario where she should have been able to ask for help. But they weren't there to help – this is what they wanted. And so instead, she was screaming at them to get away from her as she ran from them. Shortly afterwards, the police arrived, and the paparazzi led them to where Lindsay was hiding. Somewhere on her or in the car they found cocaine, and she was prosecuted.

Doctor Blunt

By my third world tour, I'd obtained the services of a tropical diseases doctor, which considering what we were picking up, seemed appropriate. The tour kicked off in North America for three months. The doc couldn't come on the road himself, but as I'd just been made an honorary Doctor of Music by Bristol University, he deemed me qualified to self-prescribe as necessary. And so, he equipped me with an expeditionary medical kit, with instructions. The inventory read as follows:

> Paracetamol – for hangovers.
> Codeine – for really bad hangovers.
> Tramadol – for on-death's-door hangovers.
> Diazepam – to relax.
> Temazepam – to relax so much you shit yourself.
> Modafinil – to perk up. (Mainly used by the sound engineer if he couldn't score any speed.)

Viagra – to perk it up.

Cialis – to perk it up for too long, in my opinion.

Acyclovir – if after being perked up, it gets itchy.

Doxycycline – if after being perked up, it hurts to pee.

Levonelle – to avoid a paternity suit.

Now, explaining to someone you've just spent three, life-changing minutes with why you have The Morning After Pill is complicated. The best line I could come up with was, 'Hey, I just happen to have one of these lying around.' The line, 'Vitamin C? One for you, one for me?' is out of the question for legal and moral reasons, however, just out of interest, I did try one myself, and had an over-emotional and quite moody twenty-four hours.

Fairly early in the tour, I had a couple of days off, so flew to Denver to write with Ryan Tedder, the lead singer of OneRepublic. I'd arrived the day before the session, alone, and it was my birthday. The record label had sent champagne and some Buffalo chicken wings to my hotel room, and so there I was, drinking champagne and eating cold chicken wings, when the phone rang.

It was Elton.

'What are you up to?' he asked.

'I'm eating chicken wings and drinking champagne on my own,' I told him.

'Great. Find yourself a date. I'm playing with Billy Joel at the Pepsi Center in downtown Denver tonight, and you're coming,' he told me.

I didn't know anyone in Denver, so I texted a friend in Los Angeles asking if he did, but having not heard anything back, headed down to the arena solo.

The Pepsi Center is an old, rundown venue in the centre of town, and like many North American arenas, was more often used for ice hockey. Elton had got me front-row seats, literally bang in front of him, in amongst the crazy fans, and close enough for he and I to be able to talk to each other through the concert. Fifty-eight minutes in, after he'd sung 'Madman Across the Water', Elton turned to the audience to speak.

Pointing a finger at me, he said in his laid-back tone, 'I want to dedicate the next song to an artist you all know called James Blunt, whose birthday it is today.'

The crowd of twenty-five thousand people erupted into 'Happy Birthday', and one of the spotlight guys swung his lamp on to me as they did. As the crowd finished, Elton plucked the first notes of 'Tiny Dancer', and the crazies in the front row beside me went berserk. Not only is the song a fan favourite, but they'd just realised who was in the front row with them, and most excitingly – that I was one of them.

A few songs later, my phone buzzed. My friend from LA had messaged to say there was a girl outside the front door of the venue waiting for me. He'd asked her to do him a favour and hang out with a friend of his from England because it was his birthday. He hadn't said anything about me other than my name was James.

When I walked outside, the girl realised, probably with horror, that the James she'd been told to meet was that dude that sang that song way back in 2005. But it was too late.

'Allie?' I asked her.

I grabbed her hand, walked her through the venue lobby, into the arena itself, down the steps, and along the aisle, to the very front row. Ecstatic, all the mega-fans reached over to hug and high-five her like we were just married, and she was part of the mega-fan family now.

A couple of hours into the show, Billy Joel climbed on the stage and did a few songs on his own. Elton gestured for us to meet him at the side of the stage, and we were swept back into his dressing room. What was normally an ice-hockey team's changing room had been dressed to look more welcoming. Black drapes hid the benches and hanging rails, while sofas, carpets and plants made it less painful to spend hours in. Behind Elton, clothes rails were packed with near identical outfits, and the tables were full of purpose-made trays of near identical sunglasses, with lenses of ever-so-slightly different shades of pink. As he got changed into a Gucci tracksuit with his name emblazoned on the back, Elton turned to Allie.

'It's his birthday, so you'd better fuck him, darling,' he joked.

'I can't stay the night,' Allie replied, bashfully.

After the encore, and a final wave from Elton, we slipped into the streets of Denver. It was freezing outside, and as we walked amongst the thousands of people all leaving the concert, everyone was calling out, 'Happy Birthday, James!' and in every bar, people came over and gave us free drinks saying, 'Happy Birthday, James!'

'This is weird,' Allie said in her West Coast drawl. 'So, like, when you're famous, not only does everybody recognise you, but they even know when it's your birthday?'

Although Allie didn't do as Elton had instructed, I woke up the next day, drove to Ryan Tedder's studio and wrote a song called 'Stay the Night'. And although it's a terrible song, and hopefully you haven't heard it, it was a massive hit on the continent. So, thanks Elt.

I flew back to join the tour in Minneapolis, and in the afternoon, my tour manager got a call from Paisley Park, which is Prince's house, saying they'd been instructed to request two tickets to the concert. For a musician, this is a huge deal. Prince was arguably the best musician and performer on the planet, so it was extraordinary that he might want to come to a James Blunt concert. Gallagher, Albarn, Weller – you can all eat your hearts out.

Tickets, VIP parking, back entrance and after-show passes were all hurriedly organised, and as we were getting dressed for the show, Bobble told us that a blacked-out limo had just pulled up at the back. In the last few seconds before we took to the stage, we played '1999' in the dressing room and all hugged each other.

'Have a good show,' we told each other.

In truth, we were bricking it. There wasn't a moment in that concert that I wasn't thinking about what he might be thinking. We played our fucking hearts out.

After the show, I had a quick shower and hurried to the afterparty room. There were a gaggle of guests there, but I couldn't see Prince. He is pretty short though. I turned to a bald man on my left who was with another long-haired, scruffy man.

'Hi there,' I said. 'Who are you?'

'Hey man,' he replied. 'I'm the gateman and he's the gardener at Paisley Park.'

Damn, I thought. *After all that, Prince is in the Weller camp.*

At the end of the tour, my five truck drivers came to see me.

They said they'd been away from home for a long time and needed to put on a good show for their wives and girlfriends when they got back, and did I have anything for that.

I pulled open the box that the tropical diseases doctor had given me. For problems such as this, the instructions simply read:

'Half a Viagra, plus a third of a Cialis – stiff enough to hang your coat from.'

A week or so later, they all messaged me, incredibly grateful, and with permission from their loved ones to go on tour whenever they liked.

Bill Clinton

I first met Bill Clinton at a private event in the Peninsula Hotel in Beverly Hills organised by Bosnian socialite Diana Jenkins. Diana had arranged a dinner for around thirty people, all of whom I could name and you would know – Jack Nicholson, Cher, Sean Penn, Guy Ritchie, David Arquette, Joaquin Phoenix, Barbra Streisand, Salma Hayek, Matthew McConaughey and so on. As I entered the white-marbled, white-table-clothed, white-flowered function room, I was introduced to the singer Cher.

'Oh my God!' she said. 'I'm such a fan! Really!' she effused. 'It's amazing to meet you. I love your work!'

We spoke animatedly for a few minutes and then, when she'd run out of superlatives, we parted ways and I headed to the bar.

They say Bill Clinton makes you feel like the most special person in the room. Well, fairly early on in the evening, a Secret Service agent came up and asked me if it was okay if the president spoke to me. I looked at my near-empty glass and said that I might pop to the gents first, but after that, I'm sure it would be fine.

When I came back, with no one else in tow, President Bill Clinton walked over and shook my hand warmly.

'James, I wanted to thank you for everything you did in Kosovo,' he said.

And then, remarkably, he broke into an extended monologue about the dangers I must have faced as a reconnaissance officer and forward air controller during the bombing campaign, and how amazing it was that I was the first NATO soldier to reach Pristina airport and face off with the Russians when they had beaten us there. All of this, he noted, when he was just in the rear with the gear. Obviously, he was well briefed, but the message felt like it was genuine and came directly from him.

'No, thank *you*, Mr. President,' I said idiotically, 'I think you did a great job too.'

It was only a few minutes, but he had indeed made me feel very special.

The president walked away and on to someone else, and Cher came skipping back over.

'I'm so sorry,' she said, 'I totally thought you were someone else.'

After dinner, President Clinton stood up and gave a forty-five-minute speech, without notes, about the state of the world. He literally linked everything, from health care to climate change to Third World debt, and how they were all intertwined. And whilst there could be no questions, as he'd completely covered everything, he finished by asking if we had any. Charged up to the eyeballs, David Arquette stood up and started ranting about how amazing we all were, and how lucky life is to have us, and isn't it incredible that this moment had us alive in it, or some other nonsense. Whatever it was that he was trying to say, a question never materialised, and as the rant went on, Bill started taking small steps backwards like Homer into a hedge.

'And another thing . . .' David slurred, before Sean Penn, equally charged up to the eyeballs, stood up, angrily waving his arms.

'Enough!' he shouted. 'We get it! We're amazing. Now, SIT DOWN!'

David Arquette sat down.

The evening ended soon after, and I watched from the far corner as Bill said his goodbyes. People nearby reached for a last handshake or gave a last bow, but as he was almost clear of the room, he turned back around, crossed the room, and came over to me.

'Hey James,' he said, 'I forgot to say, I've got both your albums. Huge fan.' And with that, he was gone.

A few years later, I was asked to play for the Clinton Foundation in London. The day before, Bill, Hillary, Chelsea and a few of us involved in the event had lunch in the Thomas Goode tableware shop on Audley Street. As a family, the Clintons were kind and engaging, and we all had pictures with them, taken by a professional photographer. My wife, Sofia, came too, which was good as she's the brains of the operation and can string a sentence together in front of these kinds of people, whereas I, as you know, am just a pretty face.

The next day, I turned up at Guildhall early for a sound check before the event. A couple of hours later, the guests started arriving – five hundred paying punters all in black tie and gowns. As the Clintons arrived, the guests lined up either side of the entrance hall and steps, hoping to catch a glimpse of them. Sofia had arrived early too, and she and I were set back behind the mass of people, but as the presidential entourage swept through the crowd, Bill saw me and called out, 'Hey James! Come with us!' The crowd parted and he reached through, grabbed my hand while I grabbed Sofia's, and together we were swept along with the Clintons into a small reception room with only eight of us in there.

Did it again, Bill, I thought. *Most special person in the room.* Anyway, I played the gig, had dinner beside Chelsea Clinton, and that was that.

A couple of weeks later, I was in New York in the *Vogue* offices. There, the famous editor, Anna Wintour, was dragging girls from all corners of the office into hers and saying, 'This is James Blunt! Tell him how much of a fan you are!' And there seemed to be an endless supply of pretty assistants, writers and assistant editors who were fans of mine for a minute if instructed to be by their boss. As this was happening, with more girls still to come, my phone rang – a withheld number. I would normally ignore it, especially in the situation, but for some reason I picked up, listened, and then turned to Anna Wintour.

'I'm so sorry,' I said. 'It's Bill Clinton.' And then as if talking to an old friend, 'Bill! Hi! How are you?'

So even when he wasn't actually there, he *still* made me feel like the most important person in the room.

Sofia Wellesley

I should tell you how I met Sofia. It was early 2010, and having burnt my bridges with girls of my own generation, my sister Daisy, who is twelve years my junior, suddenly became more useful. Daisy and I shared a little house in Chelsea, and one evening, she invited a girl round for dinner. I immediately knew that this girl was the one. Sure, she ticked all the boxes: tall, skinny, blue-eyed, blonde, with low expectation. She was also the Duke of Wellington's granddaughter, so if I married her, I'd get some kind of title. Or so I thought. As it turns out, no such title has been forthcoming – not even an Honourable, and I am left feeling a bit Nadine Dorries about the whole thing. But there was something more to her than I'd ever seen or met before. I spent the whole dinner staring at her, wondering if she knew. Anyway, I set about trying to get this girl drunk enough to find me attractive – 'Drink me pretty,' I would tell her – which in the end, took almost two years.

If I'm honest, this was a greater investment in time and alcohol than I'd initially expected. I also created an alcoholic in the process. She is the only person I know who keeps a bottle of tequila by the bed and has a shot first thing in the morning, but then again, if you woke up next to James Blunt each morning, what would you do?

In the early days, before we were actually an item, I convinced Sofia to visit me on tour. She flew in to Amsterdam, and at 1 a.m. after the concert, we all climbed on the tour bus. We had a day off the next day, so would be driving overnight to Verbier, where we had planned a day's skiing. It's a double-decker bus, with a driver's cab, small kitchen and sitting room downstairs, and sixteen bunks, small loo and sitting room upstairs. We were in the upstairs 'back lounge' having a post-Amsterdam rave, when the bus swerved to the right and we heard the 'drrrrr' of the wheels on the rumble strips on the side of the motorway. Everyone put their arms in the air and cheered.

A few minutes later, it happened again – 'drrrrr' under the right wheels, and we all cheered again.

But when it happened a third time, I slipped out of the door, stumbled down the stairs and went into the driver's cab.

The driver was new.

'Everything okay?' I asked him.

He had a thick Scandinavian accent, and this was the first time we'd met.

'Yesh!' he said excitedly. 'Ecshept . . . I she rabbitsh in the road. Big one'sh!' he explained, before suddenly exclaiming, 'There'sh one!' as he swerved to the right to avoid something only he had seen.

'Err, you haven't had any of the cake that's in the kitchen, have you?' I asked nervously.

The caterers had made us a cake with a little extra added from Amsterdam.

'Oh yesh!' he nodded. 'Two schlices!'

I went upstairs and woke Bobble in his bunk and asked him to come downstairs to the driver's cab. Bobble came down in his underpants and stood beside the driver all night, with strict instructions to tell the driver to drive through every rabbit he saw. Then I walked upstairs and back into the party and didn't mention it to anyone inside.

A year and a half later, I proposed to Sofia – and it didn't go well. I'd suggested she give up her job and come on my eighteen-month tour, but she said that, before she would do that, she'd need a ring on her finger. Nervous of the commitment – although confident she was the one – I left it until the weekend before the tour. Sofia flew out to join me in Berlin where I was doing some promo. I'd been carrying an engagement ring around with me for the last six months, but this weekend, I had also brought a padlock with our names and the date inscribed on it. My idea was that we'd have dinner, and then go for a walk. There was a bridge nearby on which lovers clasp padlocks and throw the key into the river as a sign of their eternal love. I was forty years old, and this was the biggest step towards adulthood that I'd ever taken, and I wasn't taking it well. I was desperately nervous. Through dinner, as I tried to make conversation, and was gabbling on about how marriages almost always fail, and how I didn't want to be one of those failures, rather than the ring Sofia was hoping for, I produced the padlock.

Sofia assumed I was dumping her.

By the time we got to the bridge, she was wildly drunk and in tears. In the dark October night, soaking wet from the rain, I eventually produced the ring. Sofia struggled to focus on what it was, let alone its meaning, and spent the rest of the night on the hotel floor throwing up.

Fortunately, she suffers from memory loss, so woke up with a sore head and a ring on her finger, and I told her that it had been a beautiful moment.

Things didn't go especially smoothly with her family either. I stupidly failed to ask Sofia's father for her hand in marriage, and instead, thought it would be a good idea to send him a postcard from Atlanta. Worse still, I had been given the wrong address, and so even though it was registered mail, the postcard never arrived. As a result, his wedding speech was so painfully acerbic that my new brother-in-law left the party and walked round the car park till the speech was over.

The wedding itself was in Majorca – a tiny affair for just forty friends and family – in a deconsecrated chapel. (Having signed a deal with the devil, I'm not allowed in a functioning place of worship.) And other than the paparazzi helicopter flying overhead, it was a beautifully private moment.

The next day, we had planned a large party on a beach in Ibiza for two hundred and fifty friends. My only job was to get the team of forty friends and family from Majorca to Ibiza, and rather than charter our own plane, I paid a third of the price by buying almost all the seats on the Iberia plane that flies between the two islands. I was joking about how it was an almost private jet . . . until the flight was delayed an hour.

And the joke wore thinner still when the flight was delayed two hours.

And then it was cancelled.

Mild panic set in. We asked the Iberia staff when the next plane was, and they explained that as ours was the hopper plane that goes back and forth between the islands, the next plane was our plane, and our plane was broken, so there would be no next plane.

Absolute panic set in. Waiting for us in Ibiza, as well as the seated dinner, chefs, waiters, band and DJ, were two hundred guests who had flown in from all corners of the planet – and there was every chance we wouldn't be there.

I don't know what you'd do in this situation. You'd think boats, maybe. Or hot air balloons. For a moment, I asked myself what Bear Grylls would do, but then reflecting on the last time I did that, I decided against. And then it struck me – oligarchs. I started phoning every oligarch I'd ever heard of. Literally anyone: Abramovich, Lebedev, Berezovsky – even though he'd died the year before – fuck it, all of them. While I was doing this, my best man noticed an Air Berlin flight was boarding that very minute in the other terminal. It was due to depart in the next thirty minutes so, still on hold with Berezovsky, I grabbed my new wife and her wedding dress and started running, telling my best friend that I would send instructions for him and the others as soon as I could.

Minutes later, and sweating profusely, I got to the Air Berlin gate. People were pointing and saying, 'Hey, there's James Blunt looking desperate and sweaty,' but the staff sent us back to a transfer desk. We ran back in the direction we'd come, found the desk, and approached the woman behind it.

238

'It's our wedding day, there are forty of us trying to get to Ibiza, but our Iberia flight has been cancelled. Please can you help us get on the Air Berlin flight that's boarding now?' I asked.

She looked at us looking desperately at her, with a wedding dress under my arm, and panic in our eyes, and after some thought said, 'Oh, all right – I can get *one* of you on.'

'You're amazing!' I said, 'Thank you so much! But – you do know how a wedding works, don't you? And who do you choose to go? Bride or groom?'

She tilted her head to one side and paused. 'Okay, I can get six of you on.'

All right. So, that's me, my bride, my parents, and my best man and his wife – oh fuck, not my best man and his wife – my new in-laws. Anyway, the chosen few dashed to the gate and got on the plane. I did a quick count up – there were well over fifty empty seats on the plane, but at that moment, I got the call. Oligarch Numero Uno – Len Blavatnik, one of the richest and certainly the most generous person on the planet, came through. As we were taxiing down the runway in the near-empty Air Berlin flight, I texted my best man to tell him to head to the private terminal. A plane of considerably greater luxury was about to land and take him and the rest of the travel party to Ibiza. We made it to our own wedding party with only minutes to spare.

As I'd recently sung at their wedding, we had a joint honeymoon with Elton John and David Furnish in Hawaii, except Sofia's grandfather, the Duke, died the day before, so she couldn't come.

After that, Sofia came on tour for eighteen months straight, sleeping on the tour bus with fifteen men each night, standing on the side of the stage with a full glass of champagne in one hand and an empty bottle of champagne in the other. Although the band call her Jeanine, after the divisive wife in *Spinal Tap*, she has proved more than useful on tour. Fluent in Spanish and French – and more than easy on the eye – when twenty police raided our dressing room with sniffer dogs in Quito, Ecuador, while Bobble removed the contraband, she convinced the dogs to stop sniffing and the police to confiscate only half our beer.

'We've been raided by the police!' she told me during the encore.

'What were they looking for?' I asked nervously.

'Beer!' she replied excitedly.

Along the way though, our marriage has been tested. Five minutes into the film premiere of *Stars Wars* that I was attending with Carrie, Sofia – pregnant with our eldest child – went into labour.

'Are you sure it can't wait a couple of hours?' I asked her over the phone from my seat in the Leicester Square auditorium.

Apparently, it couldn't.

But I did get my own back. During her second pregnancy, I went on tour in the US for four months with Ed Sheeran. In an act of incredible timing, Sofia gave birth the day I returned home. The next morning, I drove her and the newborn baby home, and that afternoon, in an act of even better timing, went on tour again for the next nine months. At the birth the day before, I'd been so unwell that the midwives brought a second bed into the delivery room and tended much more to me than they did to her – occasionally taking the gas and air off her to give to me.

What Sofia and the midwives didn't know was that I'd actually just been desperately hungover after Ed Sheeran's end-of-tour party – a fact I got away with for over a year, till she overheard me drunkenly regaling the actual version of events to someone at a party.

Parenting has not come naturally to me, and the mistakes I have made have had quite serious consequences. I taught my eldest to play hide and seek, but thought it might be amusing to tell him we were actually hiding from the taxman. When the doorbell at home rang, he and I would run and hide shouting, 'Quick! Hide! The taxman!'

This was all jolly until my son taught the same game to his friends at school, and someone reported it to Her Majesty's Revenue and Customs, who announced they would conduct a tax investigation, which went on for seven years.

Now, a tax investigation is boring, and explaining it is even more so, so I'll nail down seven years of back and forth with HMRC in the shortest possible way:

HMRC: How come you don't pay tax in the UK?

Me: Because I live in Ibiza.

HMRC: Your home can't be in Ibiza. That's a holiday destination!

Me: Don't be angry with me just because you chose to live in Bracknell.

HMRC: Fuck you. Listen, you fuck – prove Ibiza is your home, or we'll screw you big time.

Me: Okay, I'll try. What exactly defines a home?

HMRC: We're not telling you.

Me: My wife lives with me in Ibiza. So it's a proper family-type home. Is that enough?

HMRC: No.

Me: My clothes and possessions are in Ibiza. Is that enough?

HMRC: No.

Me: Okay. Umm . . . you don't have a toothbrush charger on you, do you?

HMRC: Err, no. It's at home. Why?

Me: My toothbrush charger is in Ibiza.

HMRC: Fuck. You win.

For real. As far as HMRC is concerned, home is where your toothbrush charger is. And with that, the tax investigation was over.

Billy

In a remarkable feat of disorganisation, I ended up getting married on the same day as my best friend Billy, and so had to helicopter out of his to get to mine. Sofia and I left just after the best man's speech – which I'd given. The part where I'd described the bride noticing me sitting on top of the cupboard in my bedroom wearing a gas mask, while she and Billy were having sex on the bed below, hadn't gone down especially well with the father of the bride, who has hated me ever since.

It didn't help that on the day of the wedding, we were still broken from the stag do. I'd taken Billy and his closest friends on the tour bus to Newmarket Racecourse, where I was playing. The race organisers had given us a box, and let Billy start a race, and in the evening I did a concert to twenty thousand people. At the start of the concert, I told the audience we were here for Billy's stag do, and when I sang a song called 'Billy', he came out dressed as a *Top Gun* fighter pilot and did a silly dance.

Before the show, I'd given him an ecstasy tablet, so at forty-five minutes in, just as he was coming up, I shouted, 'Crowd surf!' and we threw Billy on top of the audience. They passed him across the mass of people, to the very back of the crowd, and dropped him there. High and disorientated, it took him the rest of the concert to make it back to the stage.

When we finished the last song, the band and I bowed, and as we left the stage, a low rumble began to circulate through the audience.

'Billy . . . Billy . . . Billy . . .'

Louder and louder they called.

'BILLY . . . BILLY . . . BILLY . . .'

Till at last, after forty-five minutes of stumbling around wildly, he found us, ran onstage – arms aloft – and to huge cheers, took the bow.

Months after the wedding, Billy would call me asking for a sizeable loan for a restaurant he was investing in in Liverpool with his new father-in-law. I thought it was a bad idea – business and friendships don't mix – but Billy was insistent.

'This is my one shot, James. Come on,' he'd said.

I told Billy it might be the price of our friendship, but he said he wanted the money anyway, and in the end, I conceded.

I didn't see Billy for over a year after that. Then, one evening, when I was bathing my children in our house in Kensington, the doorbell rang. Answering the buzzer, I was surprised to hear my old friend's voice.

'Hey Billy. We're upstairs,' I told him. 'Come on up.'

Billy walked in, sweating and agitated. He was looking a little pasty.

'Jesus,' I said. 'Everything okay?'

He sat down at the end of the bath while I washed the children, and after a few deep breaths, he began.

'Listen, mate,' he said anxiously, 'you're not going to believe this, but the dog shat on the sofa in our rental property in Liverpool, and . . .'

'Stop there,' I cut in, already laughing. 'You're not honestly going to try to go from "My dog shat on the sofa" to ". . . and that's why I can't pay you your money back" are you?'

'Yes!' he exclaimed, with surprise.

'Well, this I've got to hear,' I replied.

To this day, I can't quite remember how he'd managed to make it all tie in, but somehow, the dog shitting on the sofa in the rental property in Liverpool resulted in his eviction, the restaurant failing and him falling out with his father-in-law – and because his father-in-law hates me because of my speech at the wedding, he's kept the money.

In fairness, I probably owe Billy the same amount of money for a number of reasons. I wrote the song 'Billy' the day he left my Fulham Palace Road flat to move in with gay Ed. I sang it at my next concert in some tiny dive in Farringdon where, as usual, he'd come to support, this time bringing his girlfriend.

The lyrics are pretty punchy:

> Billy's leaving today, don't know where he's going.
> Holds his head in disgrace. He can't escape the truth.
> He knows the price that he's paid.
> He admits that it's too late to admit that he's afraid.

Billy's leaving today, don't know where he's going.
He's got lines on his face. They tell a story of his pain.
He accepts it's his fate.
He admits it took too long to admit that he was wrong.

Once he was a lover sleeping with another,
Now, he's just known as a cheat.
Wished he'd had a mirror looked a little clearer,
Seen into the eyes of the weak.

At this point, his girlfriend stood up, punched him, and left.
So maybe Billy and I are quits now.

Ed Sheeran

Ionce slashed Ed Sheeran's face open with a sword, and blamed Princess Beatrice, and the newspapers picked up on my lie, and Buckingham Palace called, asking me to put the record straight, but when I did, Ed Sheeran's manager phoned to say that if I told the truth again, he'd throw me off Ed's tour.

True story.

So this is what happened:

I was at Royal Lodge – Prince Andrew's house – on what I guess you'd all now call a straightforward shooting weekend, and by 1 a.m. on the Saturday night, all the guests had gone to bed except me and Ed Sheeran. We were both drunk, and seeing a pair of ceremonial swords hanging on the wall, we thought it might be fun to have a sword fight. There was also a suit of armour, which we divided between us. Ed got the arms and chest, and I wore the legs and helmet. Mine was the worse combo. The heavy metal legs restricted my movement, and

247

the helmet limited my already blurred vision. Ed's a naturally competitive person, and I've always held a slight grudge against him for stealing my pop crown, so in our drunken state, the fight rapidly became more aggressive.

'There can be only one!' I screamed, as I swung the heavy sword at the Ginger Ninja – my battle name is Pop Midget – and through the slit in my helmet, I saw him flinch and drop his sword, dashing his hands to his face as he did.

I took the helmet off to see blood pouring between his fingers.

It was a sobering moment.

Ed was trembling slightly. I asked him to show me his face, and he removed his hands to reveal a two-inch cut that ran vertically just below his right eye. It was deep and bleeding heavily. I told him to apply pressure and left the room, promising to be back shortly. Two minutes later, I returned with a medical kit from the pantry, and opening it up, told him that I would do the stitches.

Ed was having none of it.

Relenting, I awoke a royal protection officer who put Ed in a car and on to Windsor Accident and Emergency. The wound required six stitches, all of which I swear I could have done myself.

We woke the next morning with hangovers, and I was obviously mortified and deeply apologetic. We said our goodbyes, and that evening, I found myself in a pub in Battersea with a few industry people – including Ed's manager. They'd seen pictures of Ed's stitched up face and wanted to know what had happened, and I foolishly joked that it was Princess Beatrice who had slashed him by mistake while trying to knight me.

I never found out who spilled the beans but, three days later, *The Sun* ran the story, except, to my horror, they went with the wrong version of events. They described in some detail how I'd suggested to Princess Beatrice that, because I pay my taxes, she should knight me. (I guess Sir James does have a nice ring to it.) They went on to describe how the princess removed the sword from the wall, and I knelt down in front of her. A crowd of house guests gathered to watch, and as Her Highness flourished the sword from its scabbard, Ed, who was behind her, flinched and consequently was dashed to hospital to be stitched up.

A few days later, I got a phone call from Buckingham Palace asking if I could shut the story down. I was about to go on a four-month tour round the States with Ed, so in interviews, I told the journalists the real version of events: Ed and I were just messing around with the swords, and that I had drunkenly tried to decapitate him in a failed attempt to regain my pop crown, and that the whole princess knighting me story was just a bad joke. For whatever reason, Ed's manager immediately called mine to say that if I repeated the Ginger Ninja/Pop Midget version of the story again, I'd be thrown off Ed's tour. I guess he must have been really married to that version of events.

Either way, I won the battle, but lost the war – Ed still carries the pop crown, but he wears a small scar on his right cheek that says, 'Blunt was here.'

Daddy's Watch

My very first memory – other than crashing the family car – was my grandfather's funeral. I remember the coffin by the altar, and how strange it felt knowing there was a body inside. Although I didn't know my grandfather well, I had a sense of his warmth. We are an old, once-aristocratic family, now faded and frayed around the edges. The watch he wore summed that history up – it was an old steel Rolex Oyster Perpetual, but rather than looking expensive, it had a simple grey cloth strap and a million scratches. As far as I know, he'd worn the same watch all his life. It was part of him. So, when he died, my father and uncle decided that he should be buried wearing it. But as they were lowering the coffin into the ground, my father had a change of heart and stopped proceedings. In a big hoo-ha, he opened the coffin and took the watch off my grandfather's wrist, and from that day onwards, he wore it instead. And so he carries a bit of his daddy with him.

Since then, I haven't ever seen my father take the watch off. It's part of him now. As it has a cloth strap, it didn't even trigger metal detectors in airports, until one time going through airport security in Ibiza, they told him to take it off. Gathering all his things together afterwards, and making his way to the gate, he suddenly realised he didn't have the watch. Blood rushing to his face, he hurried back to security, and asked desperately if they'd seen it. The Spanish security staff shook their heads unhelpfully, and my father returned to the gate and boarded the plane. Before they took off, he messaged me and asked if I would go to the airport.

Lost and Found in Ibiza airport is a joke. At the information desk, they hand you a phone and after a few rings, a faceless person with a strong Spanish accent answers. You describe to them what it is that you've lost over the phone. You don't get a face to face with anyone. The person you're speaking to asks you to hold the line for a few minutes while they look for your item – they're probably checking their Insta page instead – and they then tell you they don't have it. The process is entirely dissatisfying.

I called my father and told him I'd failed, and I know he felt like he'd lost a piece of his father again.

I got home determined to try again. I'd been to the airport a handful of times to help launch David Guetta's airport bar – which closed after just a year – but they'd used me for publicity, so I phoned a few people, and twenty-four hours later, I was asked to go back.

This time, things were different. I was led into an interview room with two Spanish policemen. I sat down across the other side of their desk, and told them a story.

251

'My very first memory – other than crashing the family car – was my grandfather's funeral,' I told them. 'And as they were lowering the coffin into the ground, my father stopped proceedings, and in a big hoo-ha, he opened the coffin and took the watch off my grandfather's wrist, and from that day onwards, he wore it instead.'

One of the policemen, Norberto, was hooked. In a rich Spanish accent he announced, 'I will find your father's watch!'

He didn't have much to go on. I told him what time I'd dropped my parents off at the airport, and that they'd both got white hair, and off he went.

And then, nine days later, I got an email in Spanish saying, 'I have your father's watch!'

I couldn't believe it.

'A woman stole it,' Norberto explained. 'I have tracked her down to the mainland, and tomorrow, we will arrest her!'

So, he didn't have the watch yet.

The next day, the police went to a woman's house on the mainland, banged on the door, and terrified at being tracked down, she handed over the watch and begged for clemency. It was the watch I was after, not her, so I didn't press charges.

When I drove to meet him at the police station in Ibiza Town, Norberto explained that he had checked the airport CCTV and seen two white-haired people pass through security just after the time I said I'd dropped them off. As my father had been doing up his belt, a woman had reached into his tray and taken his watch. Norberto had tracked her and her three friends to a gate, where she boarded a flight to Valencia. Looking through the manifest, he found a party of four, googled them, and had ID'ed the thief.

But here's where it got sticky. Spanish law doesn't allow the police to send evidence to Ibiza, or to Norberto, or to me. Without a court case on the mainland, there was no way to release the watch. But we'd dismissed the charges. This legal catch-22 went on for nine months. Norberto at one stage almost gave up – until one day he got the court to agree that I could come to the police station where the watch was being held and sign for it myself.

I hadn't told my father that I'd been on a nine-month mission to find his watch. If I had, I know he'd have been more embarrassed than anything – and perhaps he didn't want reminding of the loss any more anyway.

So quietly, I caught a flight to Valencia. There, I hired a car and drove two hours north to a small, near-empty town called Alcalà de Xivert. In the town centre was a small police station, and inside, they were expecting me. I was ushered into an office, and there, they produced a watch. My heart sank. It looked like an old Rolex Oyster Perpetual. It had a new plastic strap, the serial numbers had been shaved off the back, and it had a million scratches – all indicating it could have been my father's stolen watch – but what troubled me was the second hand. Rather than the smooth movement of a Rolex, on this watch, the second hand ticked, and anyone who knows Rolexes will tell you that means it's a cheap fake like the ones they sell on the beach.

It was the end of the road. And I was left with a conundrum – I could either walk away empty-handed or take the fake. Either way, there were no more leads and there would be no further investigation. I decided to take it, for a memento more than

253

anything else. I thanked the police officers politely, signed for the watch, and went and sat in my hire car on the street outside.

Sitting there in the middle of nowhere, holding this scuffed, valueless watch, I thought now was probably time to tell my father what I'd been up to.

'Hey, Daddy. How are you doing?' I said, as he picked up the phone.

'Hey, my boy!' he replied. 'How are you?'

'I'm well – in the middle of nowhere in mainland Spain,' I told him.

'Doing something fun I hope?' he asked.

'Well, not really – I'm actually on the hunt for your old watch.'

'My watch? I don't understand.'

'Listen,' I said. 'I need to ask you something. It's a longshot. Is there any way you can describe the scratches on the front of it?'

He seemed irritated suddenly. 'Of course I can't, Jimmy. It was very scratched. Why?'

'Well, I'm holding a watch,' I explained, 'but it's got a plastic strap, and the numbers have been shaved off the back, and I just can't tell if it's yours. I'm sure it probably isn't, but . . .'

'Well, I'll tell you something,' he cut in. 'Something that makes really old Rolexes stand out is they don't move the same way as newer ones. The thing is, the second hand on old Rolexes tick – like new fake ones.'

Well, would you look at that? I thought.

'Daddy – I've got your watch.'

As I spoke to him, he was on a small boat on the River Alde in Suffolk. He steered it to shore, went into the house, booked the next flight to Ibiza and packed his bag. The next morning, he drove to Stansted Airport and flew to Ibiza. Norberto and I met him at arrivals, and this old English colonel, who only ever shakes your hand, gave the young Spanish policeman a hug, and put his watch back on.

The Lighthouse Family

Things haven't always gone that smoothly with the police in Ibiza. In April 2009, I was in a recording session in New York with a musician called Gregg Wattenberg. He and I had never worked together before, so we were feeling each other out. Halfway through the session, Emme, who is my best friend in Ibiza, called to inform me that the lead singer of the Lighthouse Family had been arrested during a police raid on his house on the island, accused of accessing child pornography. Emme had been told by someone that the police were investigating a child pornography ring, and were going round Ibiza raiding various celebrities' houses, and apparently mine was next. She swore that the guy from the Lighthouse Family was innocent, which he was, but asked if I wanted his number, so that I could call him to get the lowdown.

At this stage, now oblivious to the stranger in the studio with me, I was pretty apoplectic at the suggestion that I might call a guy I've never met before, who's just been arrested – whether innocent or guilty – for child pornography.

'Emme,' I said, 'it's not going to look especially good when the police raid my house and ask if I know Mr. Lighthouse Family and I swear blind that I don't, but when they check my phone records, they find that he was the last person I called.'

And probably with a slight strain in my voice, I went on, 'You tell the police that they are very welcome to search my house – they'd find all kinds of contraband and weirdness, but be absolutely clear, with them or whoever else you're talking to, they will absolutely not find anything related to a child pornography ring.' And raising my voice still further, 'Tell them from me – I don't even like fucking children!'

Hanging up, I turned to Gregg, who was now looking pretty concerned as to whom he might be working with that day.

'Sorry,' I said. 'I meant, I don't even fucking like children.'

The Cotrobaşi Gang

But there is a dark side to Ibiza, and at times, I have been exposed to it.

When I first moved there, the DJ Erick Morillo was a big deal. His Tuesday night 'Subliminal Sessions' residency at Pacha was the night to go to, and afterwards, the hot invitation was to his house in the hills above the village of Jesus. He had one rule, though – only girls could come to the party. Oh, and one other – Erick chose who was allowed to leave the party and when. To this effect, he was also his own doorman, letting people in or out, and keeping the key in his pocket. He'd let me in, because I was famous, but I'd have to plead with him to let my mates in with me. Once in, the atmosphere was dark and edgy. Because of the neighbours, the glass patio doors had to remain closed. The white sofas in the white room with the white speakers blaring loudly wasn't relaxing, and there he would be, ploughing girls with drugs, so that he could fuck them. If one of my friends met a girl and they tried to leave together, Erick wouldn't allow it. He'd simply say that she wasn't leaving. The argument would go as far as me telling him that if he didn't let her go, it was imprisonment, and I'd be dutybound to call the police. He genuinely thought it was up to him, rather than the girl, if she left his house or not.

Against everyone's advice, my friend Bambi had a fling with Erick. At one afterparty, she woke up in his bed, having had sex with him earlier, and on the wall at the end of the bed, where he had twelve CCTV monitors – which is weird in the first place – she saw him on screen in the pool with three girls playing with his hard on. It was around ten in the morning when she called me, asking me to drive over and pick her up. When I arrived, she'd had to fight her way out of the house, and I met her on the street outside in tears.

I did actually do a gig with Erick in a city called Cantanhede in Portugal. It was a farmers' market, so there were pigs and tractors being sold. They then moved the pigs, let the crowd in and I came on, and after me was Erick Morillo. This surely has to get the prize for the strangest line-up ever. As I took to the stage, and shouted, 'Hola Cantanhede,' the front row all gave me a thumbs down – but if they wanted me to pronounce it 'Cantanyethe', why didn't they just spell it that way?

Still, it's not as bad as saying it's great to be in Dublin when you're actually playing in Belfast.

Anyway, Erick killed himself in 2020 having been charged with rape, and while his friends jumped to his defence saying it wasn't suicide, and he didn't rape her, if we're honest with ourselves, those of us who knew him know he was more than just a naughty boy.

And Ibiza has, at times, been personally scary too.

In January 2021, while I was in Switzerland, my house in Ibiza was robbed. They got a couple of things of value, like my great-grandfather's pocket watch, some gold cufflinks and a bayonet that I'd been given in Kosovo, but other than that, nothing of great value. If you're reading this and thinking of robbing me, I really don't own much stuff. Of the hundred or so things they did get, most of it was pretty much worthless – a chainsaw, thirty T-shirts all size Small, some fake Ray-Ban sunglasses, which I had been meaning to throw away anyway. They took a cowskin rug which my wife hated, and literally none of her possessions – so it's fairly obvious that it was an inside job.

The police looked round the house afterwards and, from footprints and glove marks, said they thought it was three people, and told me to hire a lawyer.

Two weeks later, the police stopped a known Romanian thief called Christian Cotrobaşi, who they'd seen turning around to avoid a routine drink-and-drive stop. In his car they found what looked to them like stolen goods – not mine, however. But they also found a key to a secure lock-up. In the lock-up they found a treasure trove of stolen goods, and in amongst them they found one item from my house – a remote-controlled helicopter, which I'd crashed on its maiden flight and no longer worked. It was literally the only thing I didn't want back. But it was enough to connect Christian with the robbery of my house, and he was arrested.

Christian and his brother, Eugen Cotrobaşi, make up two-thirds of the Cotrobaşi gang. Eugen is a six-foot-five beast, and his brother is a shorter, stocky thug, in his mid-forties, who I'd bet is missing the frontal lobe of his brain. They have been in and out of jail a few times, and in one burglary, Eugen took a child hostage. The final member of the gang is Eugen's rather plump middle-aged wife, who bizarrely comes out on the jobs too. At one stage, Eugen had tried to get into politics, so he's known to the press as well as the police, and for this reason, when the police arrested them, it hit the papers.

A couple of things happened at that stage – firstly, I wondered why on earth these huge Romanian beefcakes would steal my tiny T-shirts, which on them would only be crop-tops. Secondly, they now knew whose house they'd robbed and wondered why a pop star had literally nothing of value at all. Had they thought about it, they would have concluded that I don't have much stuff because I've only had one hit, but instead – when the police released them pending the trial – they decided they would come back to my house and have another look.

I have a Ukrainian housekeeper and Russian gardener who live in a little *casita* just off the main house. To a thief, you could easily think it might be a separate recording studio. Well, two weeks after the thieves were released, Ian, the gardener, and Olga, the housekeeper, woke up to hear what sounded like three people outside. They listened, terrified, for about fifteen minutes as the intruders walked across the roof and tried to open various shutters. Whoever they were, they didn't have Spanish accents, and the frightened couple were fairly sure they sounded Romanian. Ian called the police. Through hushed whispers, he explained what was happening, and when asked if they were still there, went to have a look out of the window. He found himself looking directly through the glass at two men and a woman who were looking directly back at him. Ian screamed, the robbers fled, and the police arrived all at the same time, but the house is surrounded by forest and the thieves got away.

The next morning, I spoke to a very frightened Ian and Olga. They are both in their twenties and Ian, who looks a little undernourished, wouldn't be much use in a fight. I reassured them that the ordeal was over now – the thieves had cleaned out the main house the first time, and had checked out the *casita* the second, and so by now they really knew there was nothing more of value at the house for them. We said goodbye, and I said I'd call them in the morning to check in.

Morning came and I called, but neither Ian nor Olga picked up. I tried every hour, leaving concerned messages, until eventually that evening, Ian picked up. He was not at my house, and he looked broken. In the middle of the night, he explained, he and Olga had woken to hear the same Romanian voices shouting aggressively outside, and loud banging on the windows. Thinking the men were trying to force their way in, Ian had called the police, whilst they both shouted at the intruders not to kill them. By the time the police arrived, the robbers had gone, but the damage to Ian and Olga's minds was done. They refused to stay at the property.

I hired a security team to come and guard the house for a month.

I also decided that after three visits to my house, I probably needed to be proactive. So the first thing I did was try to make contact with the robbers – through Facebook. From the press articles and pictures, I knew their names and what they looked like, so I found their webpages, changed my profile picture to all the things that had been stolen, and started sending them messages in Romanian asking if I could have my stuff back.

Through a contact in Ibiza called Simon Bushell, I also hired three large men to go round to the thieves' house and ask for my stuff back. The deal was simple – I'd pay my three heavies five hundred euros to go and speak to the Romanians, and a further fifteen hundred if they came back with any of my things. It wasn't supposed to be a violent confrontation. It's just that my things were worth more to me than they would be on the black market, so we might as well pay to get them back, whilst politely asking the Romanians not to come back to the house again.

My wife knew nothing of the plan, so I quietly signed off with Simon that evening, and had a fairly sleepless night. In the morning, I texted Simon.

'How did it go?' I wrote.

'You'd better call me,' came the reply.

I called and he gave me the lowdown. It wasn't exactly what I'd hoped for. The biggest of the three heavies was a Brazilian Hells Angel who Simon had met in the gym. After I'd signed off with him, the Brazilian had summoned Simon to Benirrás Beach for a chat. Walking along the beach, he explained to Simon that the Cotrobașis were violent motherfuckers, and that they'd probably end up pulling out a knife or something similar. The Brazilian went on to say that if they did, he'd have to break their legs – for which he would charge me four grand – or kill them – which would cost me twelve grand. To me, this actually sounded like a bit of a bargain, but Simon sensibly said that wasn't what we wanted and called the whole thing off.

When Simon got home from the beach, his phone rang. It was the Brazilian Hells Angel, who said that Simon needed to pay him a thousand euros for his time.

'But you didn't do anything!' Simon protested.

'Listen,' said the Hells Angel, 'I'm coming round now for the money. If you don't pay me, I'm going to beat you up, and then I'll beat your girlfriend up, and after that, I'll beat your two-year-old daughter up.'

In a panic, Simon ran round to his neighbour, cobbled together eight hundred euros and paid the Brazilian.

Now, I ride motorbikes, and I have friends who ride motorbikes, and one of them is an Argentinian called Román. He rides a Harley and knows everyone, so I called him and asked him if he knew the Ibizan Hells Angels.

'Sure I do, Blunty!' he said. 'I know the head Hells Angel!'

'Brilliant,' I said. 'Because I have a problem with a Hells Angel, and another problem with some Romanians, and I'd like him to fix both of them.'

So Román called the head Hells Angel, and then texted me to say he'd been summoned to the Hells Angel's house and that he'd give me a shout back in a couple of hours. When he did call back, he sounded flustered.

'Blunty, that was weird,' he told me. 'Before I could ask him anything, he said that I should tell you that he could go to the Romanians' house, but they'd probably end up pulling a knife on him, and so he'd have to break their legs – which would cost you four grand – or kill them – which would cost you twelve grand.'

Definitely weird, I thought.

'Out of interest,' I said, 'what nationality is the head Hells Angel?'

'Brazilian,' he replied.

So, as well as the lawyer, who is still in play as I write, and the security team at my house, and the eight hundred euros that I had to pay to Simon – even though it was Simon who had offered up the whole heavies plan – all of this ended up being significantly more expensive than my thirty small T-shirts.

But that wasn't the end.

Seeing my direct messages, the Cotrobaşis complained to Facebook that I was harassing them – and Facebook banned me.

The Fear

I returned to Ibiza from Switzerland with my family on 1ˢᵗ April 2021. For EU geeks, we'd spent ninety days in the Schengen zone post-Brexit – so every day more was illegal. Returning to a house that has been visited by robbers three times in our absence was unnerving, but I was happy to take control of my home again, and I had tooled up. Through Amazon Germany, I'd bought a pistol with a laser sight (okay, it only fires ball bearings, so it won't kill anyone, but if I hit you in the face, it's going to fucking hurt and you're going to want to get the hell out of my house). I'd also bought a large Rambo-style hunting knife, a taser, a fire extinguisher-sized pepper spray, some knuckledusters and some rape alarms for the girls on the property.

Three weeks after we'd got back, Ian the gardener, who was now back in the house, phoned at 4 a.m. to say we were being robbed again. He had woken to hear two people at his window trying to open the wooden shutter. I arrived at his *casita* as quickly as I could, armed with gun and knife. Ian was wearing flip-flops.

'Change your fucking shoes,' I told him. 'We're gonna get them.'

With Ian close to my shoulder, we went out looking for the intruders, and as soon as he saw any lights nearby, he would start frantically pointing and hissing, 'There! There they are!'

And I would say, 'That's Jesus's house.'

And he would kick off again, 'There! There! There they are!'

And I would say, 'Relax. That's cousin Sophie's house.'

And as we got to the top of the property, he would point to the trees and say, 'There! Their phones are lighting up the trees!'

And I would say, 'That's the moon.'

He had proper PTSD from the whole previous experience. I told him to go to bed, and I stayed up on guard.

A couple of weeks later, however, something much more real went down. At around 3.30 a.m., somewhere in the house, a large pane of glass smashed. At a guess, it was within twenty metres of where my wife and I slept, and it was close enough for us to have no time to think or dress. Naked, I threw Sofia the taser, and with gun and knife in hand, I set about clearing rooms like I was back in the Special Forces. Entering each room at speed, checking for either enemy or entry point, I checked each window systematically – see the glass, touch the glass, and move – so that I was a hundred per cent sure my mind wasn't playing tricks on me. Slightly quieter in the children's bedroom – see the glass, touch the glass, move – until I got to the last room. Bearing in mind that I know who these guys are, and compared to me they're huge, so all I've got is fucking rage, and a burning desire to stab them in the groin till they bleed out, I kicked the last door open and found . . . nothing.

I walked up the stairs to find Sofia on the landing holding the taser the wrong way round, pointed at her face. (This really annoys Sofia as she says it's not true, but even if it is, it's my fault – we should have practised.) I told her I was going to go outside to clear the perimeter, but first, as I was a little nervous, I needed a pee.

I walked into the bathroom, put the gun and knife down, and as I was standing there naked in front of the loo, I looked over my right shoulder and saw a large picture, which I had hung up with a bit of string fifteen years earlier, had fallen and smashed on the floor.

We both agreed it had been a good practice and went back to bed.

Tara and Jedward

I woke up one morning and walked into my guestroom to find my mate Will in bed with the actress Tara Reid and Irish pop twins Jedward. Stumbling back out into the sunlight, in the knowledge that this was something I could never unsee, I attempted to figure out how this depravity happened.

Will and I had bumped into Tara and the twins coming out of a restaurant the night before. Jedward, with their identical faces, were wearing identical bright blue suits and had blanched their skin with white makeup. They looked a little weird. Tara, who's an old friend, had been flown over to Ibiza from LA by a rich Arab, but had broken something expensive on his boat, and so he'd confiscated her passport till she paid him back. As a result, her holiday was spiralling out of control. Perhaps a little drunk, she'd told us that she was going to a nightclub called Amnesia, and with that, we said goodbye.

On our journey home, Will suddenly asked to be dropped off in the middle of nowhere. Now, Will's always been a little off-the-wall. The last time he'd got laid was with an older woman behind a curtain in the cloakroom of a busy bar in Switzerland – so I was instantly suspicious. After some pressure, he eventually confessed.

'I'm going to Amnesia,' he told me.

From there I'm pretty much working blind, except to say that three hours later, I got a text from Omar the Pharmacist saying he'd just arrived at Amnesia to find Will outside, alone and unable to get in, so he'd taken him in with him.

By all accounts, Tara was in the club having a tearful row with her Arab friend at his expensive table. Roman, friend of the Hells Angels, was trying to mediate whilst also trying to stop anyone getting near her, including Will. But as he said something conciliatory in the Arab's ear, Will, like a hyena or vulture or any other of those kinds of animals, stepped in and swept Tara outside 'for some fresh air'. Before she probably even knew it, they were in a taxi. But before Will could give an address, the car door opened and Jedward jumped in too. As they say, not all heroes wear capes – some wear matching blue suits.

On arriving at mine, Will must have taken them to Blunty's Nightclub, because when I went down there in the morning, I found two identical pairs of sunglasses neatly placed beside each other on the bar, a pair of identical brogues side by side below, and two identical bright blue jackets folded on a sofa. After that, I don't know how it must have played out, except to say that I guess Will never shook Jedward off, and at some point, he must have conceded defeat and ended up in bed with all of them.

The next day, at exactly the same moment, I received two messages, from two different numbers – neither saved on my phone.

The first read, 'Hi James. Thank you so much for having us. We had a lovely time in your beautiful house. Please can we do it again soon? Jedward.'

The second message read, 'Hi James. Thank you so much for having us. We had a lovely time in your beautiful house. Please can we do it again soon? Jedward.'

I saved them as Jedward 1 and Jedward 2 – but I have no idea which is which.

The Pandemic

When the 2020 pandemic hit, I was a month into a year-long tour. Concerts and public events were cancelled, and my forty-five man team were sent home. I flew to Verbier in Switzerland to find my family, and as the church bells rang across the country to announce a three-month lockdown, we dashed to the airport and got the last plane to Ibiza.

Some people had lockdown easy. Madonna did videos from a marble bath with petals and scented candles saying we were all in the same boat. I, on the other hand, spent the next sixty-eight days, eleven hours and thirty-six minutes locked up with my mother-in-law.

I'd also just bought a pub – The Fox & Pheasant in Chelsea. Before I owned it, it was grotty and we called it The Fox & Unpleasant. I bought it off the Greene King brewery when I was drunk, and what we found when we got inside was pretty disgusting. There was over a centimetre of dust on the lampshades, the white Bakelite wall switches were black with dirt, grease was oozing from every bit of equipment in the kitchen, and there were about a hundred and fifty used tissues under the landlord's bed upstairs. Worse still, it looked like Fred West had been at work in the vaults of the cellar.

So my wife and I spent the year before the pandemic renovating it – not that we knew anything about renovating and running pubs – but we knew a lot about drinking in them. I judge an establishment on its loos, so during the refurb, that's what I obsessed about. My search history for a year was just 'urinals'. At one point, I found myself in the Soho House loos in Berlin. The urinals there were fantastic, so having just used them, I took a step back and took a photo of them, and as I did, a guy walked in to see me taking a picture of a just-used urinal. To make things worse, he recognised me.

'Oh, mein Gott! You're James Blunt, ja!?' he exclaimed.

And somewhere in the world right now, there's a German guy recounting the story about 'This one time I met James Blunt in a toilet in Berlin and it turns out he's a urinal fetishist.'

Anyway, those are the urinals we have in the pub.

And then about six months before the pandemic, we opened. The council had issued us a licence specifying that I was not allowed to play there myself, but that we could play 'You're Beautiful' over the sound system at closing time to get people to leave. And then the pandemic hit, and I realised that both my choices of business were not pandemic-friendly.

So when it came to the vaccine, I was excited – not about the pub reopening and going on tour again – the way I saw it, the government was giving away free drugs, and I wanted to try them all.

Like most people in the UK, my first jab was AstraZeneca, but after that, I wanted to try some of that Pfizer or Moderna RNA shit. I tried scoring some Pfizer on the Royal Borough of Kensington and Chelsea vaccine bus for homeless people and drug addicts, but when people in the queue started asking for photographs, the nurses in the bus recognised me, and saw on the computer system that I'd already had AstraZeneca.

A week later, I visited a walk-in vaccination centre on the Golborne Road and gave them a fake name, made-up address, said I didn't know my NHS number and told them I'd never had the jab before.

'No problem. We'll just create a new NHS profile,' the man behind the counter said. 'We're giving Moderna today.'

Bingo. Moderna is the Ferrari of vaccines. Pfizer a BMW. Astra is like a Ford. Sputnik like a Lada. Although I do love a Lada.

When it came to the booster, I got my tropical diseases doctor to call ahead saying I was a test case and needed Pfizer. The nurse was a little nervous, but the result is I am the only person in the country to have had all three vaccines, and I am invincible.

That said, when I got Covid, it hit me hard.

I caught it from my brother-in-law, who had been to a fake wedding for two hundred people the weekend before. (Weddings were allowed more guests than other events during the latter part of the pandemic.) We'd been invited to the same rule-breaking party, but as Sofia was heavily pregnant, had said no. The Tuesday after, we attended a small, legally sized dinner, and it was quite a selection of guests – three pregnant people, two pop stars, two princesses, two heads of industry . . . and my brother-in-law. And we all caught the virus.

But for me, Covid did something weird. I was ill with a flu-like fever like everyone else, but nothing too bad. Then, on the sixth day, as I thought I was getting better, my lungs crystallised, and I lost the ability to speak. When I tried, I'd break into fits of shallow, slightly pathetic coughing, as if I was asthmatic. And I had one other minor issue – I was playing at the Royal Albert Hall in a week or so.

My friend Omar the Pharmacist messaged.

'MDMA,' he wrote.

I ignored it.

In the three days before the concert, still completely unable to speak and communicating by text, my tropical diseases doctor got in touch and prescribed me pretty much everything you can think of – anti-virals, anti-inflammatories, anti-acid reflux, steroids.

An hour before the show, I couldn't even say the word 'hello' when my mother arrived at my house, and she burst into tears. An hour later, I walked on stage not knowing if I would get through the first line of the first song. I'd lost four kilos, was rattling like a pillbox and was nervous, and then I opened my mouth, and bizarrely – I could sing. I couldn't speak . . . but I could sing. It's as if the Chinese made something so perfectly designed to get rid of me, but they just got the last, most important bit wrong.

The crowd at the Royal Albert Hall was ecstatic – but as it was the first full-capacity concert in the country for two years, I probably could have sung 'Happy Birthday' and they'd still have been happy.

And then after the concert, I was back to being a coughing, unable-to-speak mess.

The next night, we went to an outdoor party in Suffolk, and everyone was pointing to me, saying I shouldn't be there, coughing away like that during a pandemic. And then at 1 a.m., someone gave me MDMA, and by 2 a.m., not only was I dancing like a lunatic and loving everyone – I was also able to speak . . . perfectly.

The next morning, I was totally cured, as if new. I texted Omar the Pharmacist.

'I'm better,' I told him. 'You'll never believe what fixed me.'

'MDMA,' he wrote back. He didn't even put a question mark.

Now, guys, I know I'm only a Doctor of Music, and I know Omar isn't a real pharmacist, and I know Trump came up with some pretty silly suggestions, but I'm deadly serious.

MDMA is the cure for Covid.

South Africa

The pandemic was the beginning of the end for humanity and me. Society started to fray as the basic glue of civility was discarded in the age of digital communication. Human interactions declined. Global temperatures soared. War took hold in Europe. And worse, for me, Christmas holidays to South Africa with children and in-laws became a reality.

We'd booked ours pre-pandemic, but it was postponed till December 2022. I wasn't much looking forward to it anyway – we live in Ibiza, so why travel all the way to South Africa for Christmas with children and presents? And it was with my wife's side of the family, rather than my own. To add to the pain, the rescheduled holiday was moved to early December, so what should have been a week's trip was extended to a whopping seventeen days.

But shit went south before we'd even taken off.

The day before we flew, having voluntarily given blood, one of the travel party got sepsis and ended up in A & E. Her mother immediately bailed on the holiday, and then her sister, whose flight had been delayed three hours, panicked and bailed too. And these were the fun guys.

We flew the delayed twelve-hour overnight flight, little children in tow, and lost our first item of luggage whilst connecting in Cape Town – nothing important, just the baby's travel cot.

But we made the connecting flight – because it was delayed six hours.

While we were waiting, another member of the holiday group spotted us in the airport, and asked us why we were flying to George instead of our holiday destination of Plettenberg Bay. George is a two-hour drive away, she told us.

'Why are we flying to the wrong place?' I asked my wife.

She didn't know.

We eventually took off on the plane that was not going to where we wanted to go, but as it came in to land, the pilot hit full-throttle and, with everyone screaming, bailed out of the landing and did an emergency go-around. For me, I was excited that, although we might die, at least I'd get out of the holiday.

'Sorry folks,' the pilot told us. 'Bad fog.'

A few minutes later, he was back on.

'We're going to circle for ten minutes,' he told us. 'Hopefully a breeze will come through and clear things up enough to land.'

Forty-five minutes later, we were still circling.

Eventually the pilot piped up again. 'Hi folks. We're running out of options here, so I might just give it another go anyway.'

To give him his due, he got it down without ever really seeing the runway. It appeared as the wheels hit the tarmac. We disembarked, and seven of us squeezed into a five-seat hire car and drove two hours through thick fog to get to Plettenberg Bay, where our holiday house was. Somewhere on the flight, we'd lost the Square Au Pair, but who needs an iPad on holiday with children anyway?

'Wow!' the kids said as we eventually arrived. 'The house looks so old!'

It really did. Like an old colonial building with ivy all over the walls and corrugated iron rooves, sitting in between ancient mountains either side. I'm guessing it had been there for at least a couple of hundred years.

The owner was at the door to welcome us as we pulled in.

'How old is the house?' I asked, genuinely interested in its history.

'Oh, it's more than twelve years old now,' he replied in his deep Boer accent. 'It's bankrupted me three times and upkeep has been tricky.'

Swallows were nesting in the hallway, and as we unpacked the children's luggage, my wife found the packaging of the sex toys that had been used for the German reality TV show that had been filming in the property the week before.

'We're having a little problem with the electricity,' our land-lord told us. There are daily power cuts in South Africa, so I was expecting him to run us through that, but he was on about something different. 'I haven't paid my bill, so the generator can either heat the pool, or power the lights and oven – but not both. Your choice.'

I'd been away the week before and had arrived with dirty clothes, so I sent them out to the laundry that first night, includ-ing both pairs of jeans that I had.

They left the laundry out on the street that night and it was stolen.

It rained for fifteen of the seventeen days. Of the two sunny days, the beach was closed on the first because of a shark attack, and closed again on the second because there was raw sewage being pumped on to the beach.

'We normally stay in Hermanus,' my brother-in-law told me. 'It's much nicer there.'

'Why are we here then?' I asked.

He didn't know.

After the first week, we downsized houses to what we ended up calling 'The Crap Shack'. The house was on a main road, beside a slum, and you could see where people had climbed over the barbed wire that surrounded the house. The woman who gave me the key advised me to put on both the internal and external burglar alarms at night.

'Has it been burgled before?' I asked.

'Yes,' she replied.

'How many times?' I asked nervously.

'I can't tell you that, but they come for your laptops,' she replied unreassuringly.

Sure enough, on the second night at around 2.30 a.m., the outside alarm was triggered, and as has become quite usual in my life, I spent the next hour running round the house with a kitchen knife in just my swimming trunks, as I didn't own any trousers any more.

Christmas Day eventually arrived, but as my son got hit by a cricket bat and cut his head open just above the eye, I spent it with him in A & E. The doctor had just come from his Christmas lunch, was sweating profusely and had the shakes.

'I've stemmed the bleeding,' I told him confidently. 'I think it just needs glue and butterfly stitches.'

'He needs real stitches,' the doctor replied bullishly. 'I can see his skull.'

Under the skin on your head *is* your skull, so I'd be more worried if you *couldn't* see his skull.

'Okay,' I said, not wanting to provoke the professional. 'Do your thing.'

A child that young needs to be knocked out before you can stitch them up, so the sweating Boer began to unpack the mouth-piece and gas cylinder.

'Oh shit,' he said suddenly. 'When did he eat last?'

It was Christmas Day. I imagined that we'd all eaten around the same time.

'About two hours ago,' I told him.

'Damn,' he replied. 'The gas will make him vomit. I'll have to do glue and butterfly stitches.'

Ah, glue and butterfly stitches. Who would have thought?

The next day, I found myself in A & E again as my other child caught rubella, but as yesterday's doctor had died in the night, we had a more pleasant experience.

And then we flew home to Ibiza, where everything worked, and the sun shone, and the beaches had neither shit nor sharks, and we only got burgled occasionally.

Perhaps I'll just stay here from now on.

The End of Me

The dream was to be rich and famous. But if I'd known then what I know now, I'd have tried instead to be rich and anonymous. Because fame is a curious thing. They say that fame changes you, but it doesn't. It changes everybody else. Human beings become unable to say anything except ask for a selfie. Adults become giggling children as you walk past. People think you don't notice when you walk in a room and they nudge their friend, and whisper, 'Don't look now, but David Guetta just walked in.'

And whilst we talk about getting rich and famous, we don't talk about what happens on the other side – because on the whole, what goes up, must come down. The business is littered with bands and musicians who had their moment, and are now a distant memory. My star shone brightest, and momentarily, in the naughties. Sure, I might poke my head up from time to time. But it's been the long, ungraceful slide back down which has been the interesting bit.

'What happened to you?' is a question I'm asked often.

Well – kind of everything, I think back.

Twenty years after I stood guard at the Queen Mother's lying in state, Queen Elizabeth II died. As with her mother, people stood in line, this time for up to twenty-four hours, to file past her coffin and show their respect. On the final day of the vigil, when the organisers were telling people that The Queue was closed, I told my wife that I wish we'd joined. Off the cuff, we decided we should go, so hurriedly, we dropped our children at home, changed into a suit and dress, grabbed a bottle of wine, and caught an Uber to Southwark Park in Rotherhithe. The queue was ten miles long and we were in it from three-fifteen in the afternoon to one-twenty in the morning – over ten hours – and whilst, at its end, it was extraordinary to be back in the room where I stood guard twenty years earlier, the moment of bowing one's head and seeing the ever-so-sparkly crown atop the coffin was not the bit I will remember. It was The Queue itself, and the people in it. The miles trodden, the time given and the friendships made were the real show of respect to Her Majesty, more than the moment beside her coffin. How we'd got there was just as important as where we'd got to.

The same year, I went back to the venue where I'd played my first gig, The Water Rats in King's Cross. This time, it was to launch my 'best of' album, called *Greatest Hit (And songs I wish you'd heard)*.

The next day, I played Wembley Arena – still living the dream, folks.

In a business built around what is hip and cool, I made a career of being middle of the road – while critics shouted at me from the safety of the sidewalk. But what is that word, 'cool'? What are we even on about? What does it matter? Perhaps the reason I didn't care about it was because of my experience in the army, where we dealt with life and death – not what's cool and not cool. Life and death. And if I write songs about what it is to be alive or dead, addicted or clean, to be in love or not, well, none of these things are cool. They're reality – and most people in the world aren't cool. They deal with real life things. I don't want to be cool. I sing about the things that make us tick.

And sure, I know I've been lucky – but you create luck. It wasn't about being in the right place at the right time – it was about being everywhere, all the time. I was persistent – Sofia will tell you that. And along the way, I was helped by some amazing people: Rupert, Peter, Jonny, Billy, Nin, Todd, Carrie, Bobble, my band, my crew, my label, my sisters, my parents – my beautiful wife, to name but a few. They have carried me when I have faltered. Forgiven me when I have failed them. But mostly, they taught me that the dream wasn't really about fame or fortune at all – it's about the pursuit of happiness. And happiness was sharing the journey with them.

So here I am, back down on planet Earth, and it's all good. If my ego ever needs a little massaging, I remind myself that the name 'James Blunt' has been inducted into the annals of cockney rhyming slang, and as legacies go, I'm happy with that – and the fact that the words, 'you're beautiful' will forever be mine.

The Press

I am lucky to have always had great support from the press.
Here's what they've had to say over the years:

Daily Mirror, 10 August 2005
'The Big Stuff: Aargh. It's that Blunt' by Donald MacLeod
Does that 'You're Beautiful' song not get right on your napper?
Does James Blunt not realise that he's now responsible for
every bad, nasally singer screeching this piss-poor tune out at
karaoke? And how many imagination-free couples will choose
this dull-as-hell ballad as first dance at their wedding? Mind
you, it beats 'Everything I Do, I Do It For You'. Bring back the
bloody frog, all is forgiven.

The Sun, 18 January 2006
By Bill Leckie
Quick message in passing for the recording industry. Illegal
downloading isn't killing music. James Blunt is.

Daily Star, 30 January 2006

'Blunt truth is we don't want you'

James Blunt has been banned from the ShockWaves NME
Awards for being too boring. It is feared the ex-army bloke
would be a target for trendy rock 'n' roll types if he turned up at
the Hammersmith Palais do. So for his own safety Jimmy, 28,
has been given the red card from the guest list. A source told
me, 'The NME Awards have gained a reputation for being a bit
on the wild side. Copious amounts of alcohol are consumed and
bands are free to roam around the tables approaching whoever
takes their fancy. There was a lot of talk about James Blunt and
the Kaiser Chiefs after their BRITs nominations. But while the
Chiefs are A-list guests for the NME bash, James was considered
too dull. Some feared it wouldn't take long before some of the
gobbier rock stars hit out at Blunt.' While there's no indication
that Jimmy would even turn up to the event on February 23, it's
all rather embarrassing.

The Sun, 28 February 2006

By Juliet Lawrence Wilson

Poor Little James Blunt. He may be a highly successful singer,
but he claims to be no good in relationships. He could try singing
an octave lower.

Daily Star, 13 March 2006

'To Be Blunt' by Joe Mott

Graham Coxon thinks James Blunt, 28, is an empty vessel.
The ex-Blur axeman, 37, promoting solo album *Love Travels
At Illegal Speeds*, ranted, 'There's no humour in his music and

there doesn't seem to be much depth. It's the sort of thing you'd write on a card if you were sending flowers.'

Daily Star, 27 May 2006
'Mott on Blunt' by Joe Mott
Hmmm, James Blunt. There's been so much said about him because he has been so successful. I haven't met him myself, but I've heard he's supposed to be a really nice guy. But that song of his, 'Three Wise Men', I really can't stand. He's just sung it like a dick. His phrasing is just so annoying on that song. He just p*sses me off.

The Sun, 30 May 2006
James Blunt's songs are banned from radio station Essex FM because listeners are sick of hearing hits 'You're Beautiful' and 'Goodbye My Lover'.

The Sun, 1 June 2006
'Bluntly speaking, it's time for a ban' by Bill Leckie
Three days since Essex FM banned James Blunt from the airwaves, yet still Britain's other 753 radio stations won't see sense. So please, please put pressure on your favourite DJ to cleanse our ears of this menace. You know it makes sense.

The Sun, 24 June 2006
'Bluntly put, he's the pits' by Donald MacLeod
Did you hear about the girl who woke from a coma thanks to James Blunt's song 'You're Beautiful'? Apparently, it was to switch the CD player off. Then she went back into her coma.

I can't stand that upper-class fop! Why is it that despite having a face you'd never tire of hitting he's pulled some of the most beautiful women in the world? It's because some women (not all!) can't resist a man with a guitar who has a drippy song to sing. You can almost hear the knicker-elastic ping when he arrives at after-show parties. Then they find out he's just picked up a royalty cheque for £10 million in the States. Aargh!

News of the World, 25 June 2006
By Eilis O'Hanlon
Doctors brought round a girl from a coma by playing her 'You're Beautiful' by James Blunt. Which is ironic really, because his dreary voice has exactly the opposite effect on me.

The Sun, 15 July 2006
By Donald MacLeod
James Blunt is going to live with donkeys in Spain. That's karma for you – his ex-girlfriend had to live with a dirty pig for years.

Daily Mirror, 31 July 2006
James Blunt is now more irritating than traffic wardens and noisy neighbours, but there is good news for the star – people prefer him to cold callers.

The Sun, 3 October 2006
By Bill Leckie
James Blunt's song 'Goodbye My Lover' has become the most popular request at funerals. Which is fitting because his other hit, 'You're Beautiful', has bored thousands to death.

The Sun, 12 February 2007

'James Blunt gets on my nerves. We are not alike' by Danielle Lawler

Singer James Morrison says he is worried fans will bracket him with Blunt, who picked up two gongs, including Best Male Act, last year. James added, 'The main thing that worries me is people don't like James Blunt anymore. I can handle people not liking my music but if people stop liking you as a person that's not great. I kind of think James Blunt did a good album. It sold well but it's not my style – it's a bit wet for me.'

The Sun, 1 March 2007

By Bill Leckie

James Blunt is wanted by Los Angeles cops in a hit-and-run probe. Though to be fair, if I'd made his hits, I'd run as well.

The Sun, 25 June 2007

'James' hit the gratest'

Soppy ballad 'You're Beautiful' by James Blunt has been voted the most irritating song of all time. The single was No.1 in 11 countries in 2005, including five weeks in Ireland. Second in the poll to find the song that grates most was 'Axel F' by Crazy Frog, which was No.1 in 13 countries. Next was 'MMMBop' by Hanson, top of the Irish charts for three weeks in 1997. John Sewell, of market researchers www.onepoll.com, said: 'James Blunt isn't the obvious choice, but any song that is at No.1 for so long does start to get annoying.'

Daily Mirror, 5 October 2007

Blunt refusal – Singer James Blunt has been branded 'too embarrassing' to promote his former university. Bristol University left the singer off its list of notable alumni. A source said: 'He is just too embarrassing. Whining hits such as "You're Beautiful" may earn him a mint, but it won't inspire top students to join us.'

The Sun, 30 November 2007

'RANDOM TV irritations' by Ally Ross

4 Music Presents: James Blunt. A bad idea. 4 Music Presents: James Blunt's Head On A Spike. A better idea.

The Sun, 4 January 2008

By Gordon Smart

I say! It must be such a jolly lark being 'You're Beautiful' singer James Blunt. One can spend one's time throwing such posh parties in the Swiss Alps. The awfully super ski resort of Verbier is just the ticket. One would want a highly original fancy-dress theme and 70s rockers with afros would be absolutely hilarious. What spiffing fun.

The Sun, 25 February 2008

'Noel puts it Bluntly' by Gordon Smart

Noel Gallagher is flogging his Ibiza villa to get away from pop irritant James Blunt. The rocker has put the gaff up for sale – for £5.5 million – because it is too close to Blunt's. Lord Noel can't relax in his holiday Oasis knowing Blunt is just a CD's toss away. He is also worried about bumping into the annoying-voiced toff out and about on the sunshine island.

A pal revealed: 'Noel has been going to Ibiza every summer for years. But he wants to find a new holiday destination. He's fed up of hearing James Blunt bang on about Ibiza like he owns the place. It's taken the charm out of it for him so he's put his villa up for sale. It's very close to Blunt's place, and he says he can't stand the thought of Blunt writing cr*p tunes up the road.' Noel stands to make a tidy profit on the sale. He bought the villa for £2.5 million in 1999 from *Tubular Bells* creator Mike Oldfield. He even kept some of Oldfield's specially made carpets, which had the *Tubular Bells* symbol woven into them. The Oasis legend has spent most of his summers there since. His lovely missus Sara MacDonald also loved it. Epic. But things started going downhill after Blunt bought a nearby villa in 2006 and became one of Ibiza's most famous residents. His hit '1973' was inspired by the island's superclub Pacha, and his irritating vocals are hardly ever off local radio. At least Noel is getting a break from him at the moment. The guitarist is in Los Angeles putting the finishing touches to his band's next album. Brother Liam is also back in the States after jetting to London for his Valentine's Day wedding to Nicole Appleton. I can't wait to hear the lads' new material. Apparently it's a bit more psychedelic than previous offerings. I'm told one of the tracks is an absolute epic, featuring a 50-voice choir. Sounds mega. Of course, Noel will have to find somewhere new to relax and put his feet up after finishing the project. Sunny Ibiza is now out of the question thanks to that Factor 50 fop Blunt.

The Sun, 15 April 2008

'Not too posh to mosh' by Gordon Smart

A James Blunt gig is the last place I'd expect to see bone-snapping crowd surfing but that's what happened at a recent show in America. The tank commander broke his finger after launching himself from the stage into a sea of rampaging fans. I'd launch myself offstage too after hearing 'You're Beautiful' for the eight millionth time.

The Sun, 3 May 2008

By Donald MacLeod

Cretinous crooner James Blunt needed emergency surgery on a broken finger last week when fans mobbed him at a gig in the US. Good work people, just make sure you break ALL his fingers next time.

The Sun, 23 July 2008

'Your boat is full' by Gordon Smart

I say, what a spiffing time James Blunt has on his hols. The poshest chap in pop likes nothing more than larking with chums and a bunch of fillies on the back of a boat. Hurrah! James was letting his thinning thatch down in Formentera, near Ibiza. Two fine, blue-blooded specimens joined Captain Blunt for the Pimm's-fuelled shindig. They stripped for X-rated antics as Blunt filmed them. One guest was US actor Gary Dourdan, formerly in *CSI*, who was arrested in April after California cops found cocaine and ecstasy in his car. I wonder if the group had a civilised evening of merriment at Cpt Blunt's lodgings that evening? Ding dong, pip pip, etc.

The Sun, 3 April 2009
'K. Mo meets J. Lo' by Gordon Smart
It's a hard life being Kate Moss. Jet around the world, pose for the snappers then go for dinner with your famous friends. Yes, the Croydon clothes horse is living it up in New York for the opening of America's first Topshop store. Here she is preening with diva pal Jennifer Lopez at a flash dinner thrown by rag trade billionaire Philip Green on Wednesday night, the eve of the unveiling of his newest outpost. *Dreamgirls* star Jennifer Hudson was also at the party and treated guests to a sing-song. Shame James Blunt had to lower the tone by taking a turn on the mic.

The Sun, 28 July 2009
By Bill Leckie
An artist in Bristol made a sculpture of a horse from 10,000 CDs. Presumably he did the arse from James Blunt's last album.

The Sun, 30 December 2009
'Chump Blunt Out In Front' by Gordon Smart
What is the world coming to? Pop chump James Blunt's *Back to Bedlam* has been named Britain's best-selling album of the last decade. The posh singer saw off competition from Dido's *No Angel* and Amy Winehouse's *Back To Black* – second and third respectively. There must have been a lot of mums and grans happy to line the warbler's pocket.

I would.

Picture Credits

All images are from the author's own collection, except as follows: